A MIDSUMMER NIGHT'S DREAM

with Related Readings

A MIDSUMMER NIGHT'S DREAM

with Related Readings

SERIES EDITORS

Dom Saliani   Chris Ferguson   Dr. Tim Scott

I(T)P *International Thomson Publishing*

Albany • Bonn • Boston • Cincinnati • Detroit • London • Madrid • Melbourne • Mexico City •
New York • Pacific Grove • Paris • San Francisco • Singapore • Tokyo • Toronto • Washington

I(T)P™
International Thomson Publishing, 1998

Published simultaneously by International Thomson Limited:

ITP Nelson (Canada)   **South-Western Educational Publishing (U.S.A.)**
Nelson ITP (Australia)   **Thomas Nelson United Kingdom**

www.thomson.com

ISBN 0-17-606617-9

Cataloguing in Publication Data

Shakespeare, William, 1564-1616
      [Midsummer night's dream]
   A midsummer night's dream with related readings

(The global Shakespeare series)
ISBN 0-17-606617-9

1.   Shakespeare, William, 1564-1616.   Midsummer night's dream.
I. Title.   II. Title: A Midsummer Night's Dream.   III. Series

PR2827.A1 1998   822.3'3   C98-930160-5

Acquisitions Editor:	TARA STEELE
Project Managers:	JAN HARKNESS (CANADA)
	JACKIE TIDEY (AUSTRALIA)
	LAURIE WENDELL (U.S.A.)
Series Designer:	LIZ HARASYMCZUK
Developmental Editors:	KAREN ALLISTON, JULIA KEELER
Production Editor:	MARCIA MIRON
Sr. Composition Analyst:	DARYN DEWALT
Production Coordinator:	THERESA THOMAS
Permissions Editor:	VICKI GOULD
Cover Illustrator:	YUAN LEE
Research:	LISA BRANT
Film:	QUADRATONE GRAPHICS

Printed and bound in Canada
7 8 9 10   08 07 06 05

Contents

Features of the *Global Shakespeare Series*

Introduction to the Play: Information on the date, sources, themes, and appeal of the play, notes on Shakespeare's use of verse and prose, and common stage directions help to set a context for the play.

The Text: The *Global Shakespeare Series* is faithful to Shakespeare's full original texts. Spelling and punctuation have been modernized to make the plays accessible to today's readers. For the last 200 years, many editors have chosen to arrange and rearrange Shakespeare's words to create a consistent iambic pentameter in the text. For example, a dialogue involving short speeches would look like this:

THESEUS: Call Philostrate.
PHILOSTRATE: Here, mighty Theseus.

Together the three lines make up ten syllables. In some cases, editors have even taken words from one line and combined them with words from another line to create the iambic pentameter pattern. Shakespeare did not do this in his original text. The *Global Shakespeare Series* has not adopted this convention. What you see is what Shakespeare wrote.

Dramatis Personae: The list of characters is organized by families or by loyalty affiliations.

Scene Summaries: Brief synopses help you to follow and anticipate developments in the plot.

Artwork and Graphics: Original artwork has been created and designed for this series by internationally acclaimed artists.

Marginal Notes: Generous notes define difficult or archaic vocabulary. In some cases, entire sentences of Shakespeare are paraphrased into modern idiom—these are identified with quotation marks.

Notes of Interest: Longer notes provide background information on Shakespeare's times or interesting interpretations of various speeches or characters.

Quotable Notables: Brief comments on various aspects of the play by authors, celebrities, and highly regarded literary critics and professors are included. The views do not necessarily reflect the views of the editors; they are merely springboards for discussion, debate, and reflection.

Related Reading References: These references indicate that there is a piece of literature in the latter part of the book that relates well to a specific scene or speech.

Considerations: Each Act is followed by a series of scene-specific "considerations." Some involve analysis and interpretation; others will offer opportunities to be creative and imaginative.

Related Readings: The second half of the text contains poems, short stories, short drama, and nonfiction pieces that are directly related to the play. These can be read for enjoyment or for enrichment. They emphasize the continuing relevance of Shakespeare in today's society.

Ten Challenging Questions: These questions are ideal for developing into research or independent study projects.

Introduction to
A Midsummer Night's Dream

— ❧ —

Shakespearean Comedy

Many students know Shakespeare as the author of tragedies. Yet, fully a third of his thirty-seven plays are comedies. He was considered the best writer of his day for this particular genre.

Today, people think of a comedy as a work that makes them laugh. However, in the classical sense (and the one Shakespeare understood), a comedy is simply a work that ends happily. Many of Shakespeare's comedies—and *A Midsummer Night's Dream* is no exception—deal with serious themes. Even the more serious comedies, however, have bright, comical moments, hilarious characters, and witty dialogue.

The happy endings in comedies usually involve marriage or the reconciliation of lovers. *A Midsummer Night's Dream* is remarkable in that it ends with the marriage of three couples.

A Midsummer Night's Dream

A *Midsummer Night's Dream* is Shakespeare's most popular comedy and, if school productions are included, is by far the most often performed of Shakespeare's plays. What accounts for its popularity?

Perhaps the success of this play is due to its intricate plot and wide assortment of memorable characters. The story opens in the court of Theseus, a great Greek mythological hero, who is about to marry Hippolyta, the queen of the Amazons. Shakespeare then introduces two sets of lovers who, for one reason or another, are unhappy with their situation. The scene then changes to the home of a carpenter, where an unlikely crew of tradespeople are planning an entertainment for the wedding celebrations of Theseus. Leaving the world of mortals, the play enters a moonlit forest kingdom inhabited by fairies and ruled by Oberon and Titania, king and queen of the fairies. All the characters converge in this forest, with a result that is fiercely farcical and chaotically comic.

One reason for the play's success is that it works on many levels. On one level, it can be seen as a light fantasy, a comedy whose purpose is to entertain. On another level, it can be considered an elaborate allegory in which the dark forest represents the labyrinth of the unconscious through which the lovers must find their way. Some see the play as a treatise on the various forms of love.

Some scholars identify political satire within the play. They believe, for example, that the play pokes fun at King James of Scotland through the character of Bottom. As evidence they cite the arrangement that James made in 1594 to have a lion pull the baptismal cart during the celebrations marking the christening of his son. He changed his mind before the event, however, believing that a lion would frighten the women "out of their wits," and replaced the animal with a Moor. This topical allusion would have been popular in England at the time the play was first being performed because of anti-Scottish sentiments then prevalent.

A Midsummer Night's Dream continues to be popular because of its language. The play abounds in lyric poetry and song. The verse is relatively simple but elegant. The images are precise yet haunting, as when the new moon is described as "a silver bow, / New-bent in heaven."

Whatever the reasons—complex plot, unforgettable characters, allegorical significance, topical allusions, or delightful and rich language—*A Midsummer Night's Dream* continues to cast its spell and perform its magic for readers and audiences all over the world.

Title of the Play

The words of Theseus in Act Four indicate that the action of the play occurs around May 1st or May Day, and yet the title refers to Midsummer Eve, which falls on June 23rd and marks the shortest night of the year. In England, during Shakespeare's day, this was a time of festivals and frivolity. The play takes its title from this day because of the madness and merrymaking that is often associated with the midsummer festivities.

Five Plots

The action of the play begins and ends in the palace of Theseus, and all the scenes in between are organized to create a perfect symmetry.

There are five fully developed plots in the play. The preparation and celebration for the wedding of Theseus and Hippolyta serve to frame the play. The story of the four lovers occupies most of the action throughout the play. Much of the low comedy comes through the scenes involving the rude mechanicals. The fairyland sequence deals with the initial dispute and final reconciliation between Titania and Oberon. And the play within the play features the most lamentable comedy of Pyramus and Thisbe.

Confusion and chaos are the rule in the mad world of *A Midsummer Night's Dream*. A reader can only agree with Puck when he utters one of the most memorable lines in the play: "Lord, what fools these mortals be."

Belief in Fairies

Today, people think of fairies as harmless and benevolent—attractive, fragile creatures who use their magic to help needy individuals. This was not always the case.

In Shakespeare's day, the belief in the existence of fairies was considered a superstition of the distant past. Nevertheless, the folklore and traditions associated with fairies were still very strong in people's minds and imaginations. Before Shakespeare's time, people believed that fairies were essentially evil and to be feared. Parents did everything they could to protect themselves and their children from them. Stories were told about how fairies stole human children in the middle of the night and substituted for them their own deformed and grotesque offspring. Such substitutions were called "changelings," a term that Shakespeare uses incorrectly in the play.

This view of fairies as malevolent creatures, however, has changed dramatically, largely because of Shakespeare's depiction of them. He made popular the notion that fairies were amiable to humans and friends to lovers. Fairies appear or are mentioned in a number of Shakespeare's plays, including *The Merry Wives of Windsor*, *Romeo and Juliet*, and *The Tempest*.

Sources of the Play

Shakespeare used a number of sources in creating *A Midsummer Night's Dream*. For the framing story of Theseus, he consulted Plutarch's *Lives of the Noble Grecians and Romans* (1579) and Geoffrey Chaucer's "The Knight's Tale" from *The Canterbury Tales* (1387–1400).

For details of the Pyramus and Thisbe plot, Shakespeare's primary source was Ovid's *Metamorphoses* translated by Arthur Golding (1566).

John a Kent and John a Cumber (1590) by Anthony Munday appears to be the source for the fairy sequence, and Reginald Scot's *Discoverie of Witchcraft* (1584) contains much of the information used in the representation of Puck.

It has been said that Shakespeare never invented a single plot and that all of his stories are basically treatments of older works. Although this may be true to a certain degree, Shakespeare was the master of the transformational art of turning old stories into vibrant new presentations— masterpieces that have stood the test of time. *A Midsummer Night's Dream* is no exception.

Date and Text of the Play

Most scholars agree that the play was first written and performed at the wedding celebrations of a nobleman and woman. What scholars cannot agree on is the identity of the wedding party. It also seems likely that Queen Elizabeth attended the wedding. Many scholars have hypothesized that the play was performed on January 26, 1595, at the wedding of William Stanley, Earl of Derby, to Elizabeth Vere, daughter of the Earl of Oxford.

Detail of an interlude being performed at a wedding feast from a painting of the life of Sir Henry Unton, artist unknown, circa 1596.

Some scholars have suggested that Shakespeare wrote the play as early as 1592 and revised it twice, specifically in 1595 and again in 1598. Variations in the play's style in a number of places suggest revisions over a period of time.

Shakespeare wrote at least thirty-seven plays. Of these, eighteen appeared in *quarto* form. A quarto is a book that is produced by folding a large sheet into four and then binding the sheets. The result would be a book about the size of today's paperbacks.

A Midsummer Night's Dream first appeared in quarto form in 1600. In 1619, a second quarto appeared, which was basically a reprint of the first edition.

In 1623, the complete works of Shakespeare appeared in a single volume known as the First Folio. A *folio* is a book produced by folding large printed sheets in half and then binding the sheets. The First Folio edition is for the most part a reprint of the Second Quarto, but it does include a number of stage directions not found in the earlier editions.

The First Quarto, which is considered the most authoritative of the three texts, forms the basis of this edition.

Title page of *A Midsummer Night's Dream* from the First Quarto, 1600

A MIDSOMMER NIGHTS DREAME.

Enter Theseus, Hippolita, *with others.*

Theseus.

Ow faire *Hippolita*, our nuptiall hower
Draws on apase : fower happy daies bring in
An other Moone: but oh, me thinks, how flow
This old Moone waues! She lingers my defires,
Like to a Stepdame, or a dowager,
Long withering out a yong mans reuenewe.
Hip. Fower daies will quickly fteepe themfelues in night:
Fower nights will quickly dreame away the time:
And then the Moone, like to a filuer bowe,
Now bent in heauen, fhall beholde the night
Of our folemnities.
The. Goe *Philoftrate*,
Stirre vp the *Athenian* youth to merriments,
Awake the peart and nimble fpirit of mirth,
Turne melancholy foorth ro funerals:
The pale companion is not for our pomp.
Hyppolita, I woo'd thee with my fword,
And wonne thy loue, doing thee iniuries:
But I will wed thee in another key,
With pompe, with triumph, and with reueling.
Enter Egeus *and his daughter* Hermia, *and* Lyfander
and Helena, *and* Demetrius.
Ege. Happy be *Thefeus*, our renowned duke.
The. Thankes good *Egeus*. Whats the newes with thee?
Ege. Full of vexation, come I , with complaint

A2   A-

First page of *A Midsummer Night's Dream* from the First Quarto, 1600

Shakespeare's Verse

Many students find Shakespeare difficult to read and understand. They often ask whether or not the Elizabethans really spoke the way Shakespeare's characters do. The answer is, of course, no. Shakespeare wrote using a poetic form known as *blank verse*. This produces an elevated style of speech that would have been very different from everyday speech during the Elizabethan period.

Furthermore, the blank verse contains a rhythm pattern known as *iambic pentameter*. This means that most lines contain five feet (pentameter) and each foot contains an unstressed and a stressed syllable (an iamb). In other words, as Shakespeare wrote, playing in the back of his mind was a rhythm pattern that would sound like this:

da DA da DA da DA da DA da DA

The first line of the play would look like this in terms of stressed and unstressed syllables:

~ / ~ / ~ / ~ / ~ /
Now fair Hippolyta, our nuptial hour

Much of the play is written in blank verse, but the scenes involving discussions about love are written almost entirely in rhyming couplets. These "rhyming" scenes suggest to scholars that the play was written fairly early in Shakespeare's career and was later revised.

A Midsummer Night's Dream is approximately 2150 lines long, and, of these, almost 400 are written in prose. Prose contrasts strongly with the elevated style of blank verse. In Shakespeare's plays, prose is generally used in letters and other documents, in scenes involving servants and members of the lower classes, in scenes involving madness, and in scenes of comic relief. If servants are speaking nobly, however, they may use verse; and if nobles are chatting informally, they may use prose.

Keep track of when blank verse and prose are used. Notice that Theseus and the nobles speak almost exclusively in blank verse, but use prose as they watch the performance of Pyramus and Thisbe during the wedding party. This serves as a contrast to the exaggerated elevated speech of the mechanicals' play.

Reading Shakespeare

Did you know that in Shakespeare's day, there was no rule book for grammar? There was little consistency in punctuation and spelling among writers and printing houses.

It should also be noted that Shakespeare used colons and commas to cue actors and readers where to pause and what words to emphasize.

This edition retains many of Shakespeare's original commas that we would consider unnecessary today. Use the commas to help you with your reading.

Stage Directions

Shakespeare used stage directions sparingly in his plays. Because he was directly involved in the production of the plays, there was little need to record the stage directions.

In this edition, the stage directions that appear in italics are Shakespeare's. Directions that are included in square brackets [ ] have been added by the editor. A long dash "—" in a speech indicates that the speaker is addressing someone other than the person to whom the actor was first speaking.

The following stage directions appear frequently in Shakespeare's plays:

Above, aloft – a speech or scene played in the balcony above the stage level or from higher up in the loft

Alarum – a loud shout, a signal call to arms

Aside – spoken directly to the audience or to a specified character and not heard by the others on the stage

Below, beneath – a speech or scene played from below the surface of the stage using a trap-door

Exit – the actor leaves the stage

Exeunt – the actors leave the stage

Falls – the actor is wounded and falls

Flourish – a fanfare of trumpets, usually announcing the entrance of royalty

Hautboys – musicians enter playing wind instruments

Manent – the actors remain

Omnes – all

Sennet – a trumpet call announcing the entrance of a royal procession

Severally – the actors enter from, or exit in, different directions

Winding of horns – horns are sounded off-stage

Within – words spoken off-stage in what the audience would assume is an unseen room, corridor, or the outdoors

A performance at the Globe Theatre

Introduction to *A Midsummer Night's Dream*

Dramatis Personae

Court of the Duke of Athens:

THESEUS Duke of Athens, betrothed to Hippolyta

HIPPOLYTA Queen of the Amazons, betrothed to Theseus

EGEUS Noble and father to Hermia

PHILOSTRATE Master of the revels to Theseus

Attendants on Theseus and Hippolyta

Lovers:

HERMIA Daughter to Egeus, in love with Lysander

HELENA In love with Demetrius, but not loved by him

LYSANDER In love with and loved by Hermia

DEMETRIUS In love with Hermia, but not loved by her

Cast of Pyramus and Thisbe:

PETER QUINCE A carpenter, speaks the Prologue

NICK BOTTOM A weaver, plays Pyramus

FRANCIS FLUTE A bellows-mender, plays Thisbe

SNUG A joiner, plays Lion

TOM SNOUT A tinker, plays Wall

ROBIN STARVELING A tailor, plays Moonshine

Fairy Kingdom:

OBERON King of the fairies

TITANIA Queen of the fairies

PUCK Robin Goodfellow and servant to Oberon

PEASEBLOSSOM
COBWEB
MOTH
MUSTARDSEED
} Fairies, attending Titania

Other fairies attending to Oberon

Scene: Athens, and a wood near it

Act One
Scene 1

Athens. The palace of Theseus.

Theseus and Hippolyta talk of their wedding, which will take place in four days. The enraged Egeus brings to Duke Theseus his case against his daughter, Hermia, who loves Lysander and refuses to marry her father's choice, Demetrius. Theseus agrees to invoke the law of Athens, one of whose options is death for Hermia. Lysander and Hermia decide to elope the following evening. They tell their plan to Helena, who loves Demetrius. She determines to tell Demetrius of the elopement.

Enter Theseus, Hippolyta, Philostrate, and Attendants.

THESEUS: Now fair Hippolyta, our nuptial hour
　　Draws on apace. Four happy days bring in
　　Another moon. But O, methinks, how slow
　　This old moon wanes! She lingers my desires,
　　Like to a step-dame or a dowager,
　　Long withering out a young man's revenue.
HIPPOLYTA: Four days will quickly steep themselves in night.
　　Four nights will quickly dream away the time,
　　And then the moon, like to a silver bow,
　　New-bent in heaven, shall behold the night　　　　10
　　Of our solemnities.
THESEUS: Go, Philostrate,
　　Stir up the Athenian youth to merriments.
　　Awake the pert and nimble spirit of mirth.
　　Turn melancholy forth to funerals.
　　The pale companion is not for our pomp.

[Exit Philostrate.]

　　Hippolyta, I woo'd thee with my sword,
　　And won thy love, doing thee injuries;
　　But I will wed thee in another key,
　　With pomp, with triumph, and with revelling.　　　　20

*Enter Egeus and his daughter Hermia, and Lysander
and Demetrius.*

2. *Draws on apace* – approaches quickly
4. *wanes* – fades
4. *lingers* – delays
5 – 6. Theseus compares himself to an impatient young man whose inheritance is slowly being depleted by his stepmother or widowed mother (*dowager*).
7. *steep* – dissolve; immerse
11. *solemnities* – formal wedding ceremonies
14. *pert* – lively
16. *pale companion* – melancholy fellow
18. According to legend, the Amazons were a warrior race of women. Theseus' *injuries* include defeating Hippolyta, Queen of the Amazons, in a battle that ended the Amazons' attempt to conquer Greece, and then taking her captive.
20. *triumph* – festivities

23. *vexation* – troubles
25. *Stand forth* – step
forward

28. *bewitched* – Today
bewitched has a relatively
harmless connotation, but in
Shakespeare's time, it meant
literally "used witchcraft or
magic charms." An accusation
of bewitching would have
indeed been serious.

32. *faining* – softly singing
32. *feigning* – false
33. "And made a lasting
impression on her imagi-
nation"
34. *gawds, conceits* – fancy
toys and articles
35. *nosegays, sweetmeats* –
flower bouquets, delicacies
35 – 36. *messengers ...
youth* – tokens that can
strongly influence inexperienced young people
37. *filched* – stolen
42. *privilege* – right
46. *Immediately provided* –
clearly granted
49. *composed* – created
56. *kind* – matter
56. *wanting* – lacking

RELATED READING

*Theseus and the Unhappy
Man* – fiction by Robert
Watson (page 103)

64. *beseech* – humbly ask

EGEUS: Happy be Theseus, our renowned Duke.
THESEUS: Thanks, good Egeus. What's the news with thee?
EGEUS: Full of vexation come I, with complaint
    Against my child, my daughter Hermia.
    Stand forth, Demetrius. My noble lord,
    This man hath my consent to marry her.
    Stand forth, Lysander. And my gracious Duke,
    This man hath bewitched the bosom of my child.
    Thou, thou, Lysander, thou hast given her rhymes,
    And interchanged love tokens with my child.   30
    Thou hast by moonlight at her window sung
    With faining voice verses of feigning love,
    And stolen the impression of her fantasy.
    With bracelets of thy hair, rings, gawds, conceits,
    Knacks, trifles, nosegays, sweetmeats — messengers
    Of strong prevailment in unhardened youth —
    With cunning hast thou filched my daughter's heart,
    Turned her obedience, which is due to me,
    To stubborn harshness. And, my gracious Duke,
    Be it so, she will not here, before your Grace,   40
    Consent to marry with Demetrius,
    I beg the ancient privilege of Athens.
    As she is mine, I may dispose of her,
    Which shall be, either to this gentleman
    Or to her death, according to our law
    Immediately provided, in that case.
THESEUS: What say you, Hermia? Be advised, fair maid.
    To you, your father should be as a god,
    One that composed your beauties, yea and one,
    To whom you are but as a form in wax,   50
    By him imprinted, and within his power,
    To leave the figure, or disfigure it.
    Demetrius is a worthy gentleman.
HERMIA: So is Lysander.
THESEUS: In himself he is,
    But in this kind, wanting your father's voice,
    The other must be held the worthier.
HERMIA: I would my father looked but with my eyes.
THESEUS: Rather your eyes must, with his judgment look.
HERMIA: I do entreat your Grace, to pardon me.   60
    I know not by what power, I am made bold,
    Nor how it may concern my modesty
    In such a presence here to plead my thoughts.
    But I beseech your Grace, that I may know

The worst that may befall me in this case,
If I refuse to wed Demetrius.

THESEUS: Either to die the death, or to abjure
For ever the society of men.
Therefore, fair Hermia, question your desires,
Know of your youth, examine well your blood,   70
Whether, if you yield not to your father's choice,
You can endure the livery of a nun,
For aye to be in shady cloister mewed,
To live a barren sister all your life,
Chanting faint hymns to the cold fruitless moon.
Thrice-blessed they that master so their blood,
To undergo such maiden pilgrimage.
But earthlier happy is the rose distilled,
Than that which, withering on the virgin thorn,
Grows, lives, and dies, in single blessedness.   80

HERMIA: So will I grow, so live, so die, my lord,
Ere I will yield my virgin patent up
Unto his lordship, whose unwished yoke
My soul consents not to give sovereignty.

THESEUS: Take time to pause, and by the next new moon —
The sealing-day betwixt my love and me,
For everlasting bond of fellowship,
Upon that day either prepare to die,
For disobedience to your father's will,
Or else to wed Demetrius, as he would,   90
Or on Diana's altar to protest
For aye, austerity and single life.

DEMETRIUS: Relent, sweet Hermia, and Lysander, yield
Thy crazed title to my certain right.

LYSANDER: You have her father's love, Demetrius.
Let me have Hermia's. Do you marry him.

EGEUS: Scornful Lysander, true, he hath my love,
And what is mine my love shall render him.
And she is mine, and all my right of her
I do estate unto Demetrius.   100

LYSANDER: I am, my lord, as well derived as he,
As well possessed. My love is more than his,
My fortunes every way as fairly ranked,
If not with vantage, as Demetrius,
And, which is more than all these boasts can be,
I am beloved of beauteous Hermia.
Why should not I then prosecute my right?
Demetrius, I'll avouch it to his head,

---

67. *abjure* – renounce; give up

70. *Know of* – think about

72. *livery of a nun* – clothing or life of a nun. According to legend, Theseus lived around 1200 B.C.E. Nuns first appeared in Europe 2400 years later, during the Middle Ages. This is an anachronism—a detail outside of its proper time period. The combination of two time periods emphasizes the timelessness of the play's action.

73. *aye* – ever

73. *cloister, mewed* – convent, confined

78. *distilled* – plucked and used to create perfume

80. *single blessedness* – celibacy; chastity

82. "Before I give up my right to remain a virgin"

83. *yoke* – The *yoke*, a wooden bar used to control oxen, is a symbol of constraint.

yoke

86. *sealing-day* – day upon which the wedding contract is sealed

91. *Diana* – Roman goddess of hunting and chastity, traditionally associated with the moon

100. *estate* – give

102. *well possessed* – rich

108. *avouch ... head* – say it to his face

109. *Made love to* – courted;
wooed
111. *dotes in idolatry* –
worships entirely; is compul-
sively infatuated
112. *spotted* – blemished;
immoral

"Helena's father doesn't
seem to be an important
figure. I think he is a man
without political and
financial means, the
opposite of Egeus … He
has no power to ask
Theseus for a solution to
his daughter's situation."
– Cristina Keunecke, English
researcher and scholar

118. *schooling* – instructions;
information
119. *arm* – prepare
122. *extenuate* – mitigate;
weaken the power of

122. Theseus claims that he
has no choice but to uphold the
law. Perhaps he adds this for the
sake of Hippolyta, who has been
silent throughout this exchange.

127. *Against* – in preparation
for
133. *Beteem* – grant; pour
down on
134. *aught* – anything
137. *blood* – rank; parentage
138. "Oh most unfortunate! To
be too high-born to be bound
to one so humbly born."
139. *misgraffed* – poorly
matched
141. *friends* – relatives
143. *sympathy* – agreement
147. *collied* – blackened
148. *spleen* – fit of angry
passion

Made love to Nedar's daughter, Helena,
And won her soul, and she, sweet lady, dotes, 110
Devoutly dotes, dotes in idolatry,
Upon this spotted and inconstant man.
THESEUS: I must confess that I have heard so much,
And with Demetrius thought to have spoke thereof;
But, being over-full of self-affairs,
My mind did lose it. But Demetrius come,
And come Egeus, you shall go with me.
I have some private schooling for you both.
For you, fair Hermia, look you arm yourself,
To fit your fancies to your father's will, 120
Or else the law of Athens yields you up
Which by no means we may extenuate,
To death, or to a vow of single life.
Come my Hippolyta, what cheer my love?
Demetrius and Egeus go along.
I must employ you in some business
Against our nuptial, and confer with you
Of something, nearly that concerns yourselves.
EGEUS: With duty and desire, we follow you.

Exeunt all but Lysander and Hermia.

LYSANDER: How now my love? Why is your cheek so pale? 130
How chance the roses there do fade so fast?
HERMIA: Belike for want of rain, which I could well
Beteem them, from the tempest of my eyes.
LYSANDER: Ay me! For aught that ever I could read,
Could ever hear by tale or history,
The course of true love never did run smooth,
But, either it was different in blood —
HERMIA: O cross! Too high to be enthralled to low.
LYSANDER: Or else misgraffed, in respect of years —
HERMIA: O spite! Too old to be engaged to young. 140
LYSANDER: Or else, it stood upon the choice of friends,—
HERMIA: O hell! To choose love by another's eyes.
LYSANDER: Or, if there were a sympathy in choice,
War, death, or sickness did lay siege to it,
Making it momentary as a sound,
Swift as a shadow, short as any dream,
Brief as the lightning in the collied night,
That, in a spleen, unfolds both heaven and earth,
And ere a man hath power to say, "Behold!"

The jaws of darkness do devour it up: 150
So quick bright things come to confusion.

HERMIA: If then true lovers have been ever crossed,
It stands as an edict in destiny.
Then let us teach our trial patience,
Because it is a customary cross,
As due to love as thoughts, and dreams, and sighs,
Wishes, and tears, poor fancy's followers.

LYSANDER: A good persuasion. Therefore hear me, Hermia.
I have a widow aunt, a dowager,
Of great revenue, and she hath no child.   160
From Athens is her house remote, seven leagues,
And she respects me, as her only son.
There, gentle Hermia, may I marry thee,
And to that place, the sharp Athenian law
Cannot pursue us. If thou lovest me, then
Steal forth thy father's house, tomorrow night,
And in the wood, a league without the town,
Where I did meet thee once with Helena,
To do observance to a morn of May,
There will I stay for thee.   170

HERMIA: My good Lysander,
I swear to thee, by Cupid's strongest bow,
By his best arrow, with the golden head,
By the simplicity of Venus' doves,
By that which knitteth souls, and prospers loves,
And by that fire which burned the Carthage queen
When the false Trojan under sail was seen,
By all the vows that ever men have broke,
In number more than ever women spoke,
In that same place thou hast appointed me,   180
Tomorrow truly will I meet with thee.

LYSANDER: Keep promise love. Look, here comes Helena.

Enter Helena.

HERMIA: God speed fair Helena! Whither away?
HELENA: Call you me fair? That fair again unsay.
Demetrius loves your fair. O happy fair!
Your eyes are lodestars, and your tongue's sweet air
More tuneable than lark to shepherd's ear,
When wheat is green, when hawthorn buds appear.
Sickness is catching. O, were favour so,
Yours would I catch, fair Hermia, ere I go.   190

---

153. *edict* – order; law
154. *trial* – suffering

157. *fancy* – love
158. *persuasion* – advice
161. *seven leagues* – A league is approximately three miles or 4 km.
167. "To perform the May Day rituals"
168. *stay* – wait

172. According to Roman mythology, anyone (god or mortal) struck with Cupid's gold-tipped arrows will fall instantly in love.
174. *simplicity* – innocence
174. *Venus' doves* – The chariot of Venus, the goddess of love, was often depicted as drawn by silver doves.
176 – 77. Dido, Queen of Carthage, fell in love with the Trojan Aeneas. When he sailed away and left her, she was so grief stricken that she committed suicide by throwing herself on a funeral pyre.

183. *fair* – beautiful

186. *lodestars* – stars by which sailors could navigate.
186. *air* – song
187. *tuneable* – melodic
189. *favour* – attractiveness

Act One • Scene 1

My ear should catch your voice, my eye your eye,
My tongue should catch your tongue's sweet melody.
Were the world mine, Demetrius being bated,
The rest I'd give to be to you translated.
O, teach me how you look, and with what art
You sway the motion of Demetrius' heart.

HERMIA: I frown upon him, yet he loves me still.

HELENA: O that your frowns would teach my smiles such skill.

HERMIA: I give him curses, yet he gives me love.

HELENA: O that my prayers could such affection move.　　200

HERMIA: The more I hate, the more he follows me.

HELENA: The more I love, the more he hateth me.

HERMIA: His folly, Helena, is no fault of mine.

HELENA: None, but your beauty. Would that fault were mine!

HERMIA: Take comfort. He no more shall see my face.
Lysander and myself will fly this place.
Before the time I did Lysander see,
Seemed Athens as a paradise to me.
O then, what graces in my love do dwell,
That he hath turned a heaven unto a hell!　　210

LYSANDER: Helen, to you our minds we will unfold.
Tomorrow night, when Phoebe doth behold
Her silver visage in the watery glass,
Decking with liquid pearl the bladed grass,
A time that lovers' flights doth still conceal,
Through Athens' gates have we devised to steal.

HERMIA: And in the wood, where often you and I,
Upon faint primrose beds, were wont to lie,
Emptying our bosoms, of their counsel sweet,
There my Lysander and myself shall meet,　　220
And thence from Athens turn away our eyes,
To seek new friends and stranger companies.
Farewell, sweet playfellow, pray thou for us,
And good luck grant thee thy Demetrius.
Keep word Lysander; we must starve our sight
From lovers' food, till morrow deep midnight.

Exit Hermia.

LYSANDER: I will, my Hermia. Helena, adieu.
As you on him, Demetrius dote on you!

Exit Lysander.

HELENA: How happy some o'er other some can be!
          Through Athens I am thought as fair as she.   230
          But what of that? Demetrius thinks not so.
          He will not know, what all, but he do know.
          And as he errs, doting on Hermia's eyes,
          So I, admiring of his qualities.
          Things base and vile, holding no quantity,
          Love can transpose to form and dignity.
          Love looks not with the eyes, but with the mind,
          And therefore is winged Cupid painted blind.
          Nor hath Love's mind of any judgment taste.
          Wings and no eyes figure unheedy haste.   240
          And therefore is Love said to be a child,
          Because in choice he is so oft beguiled.
          As waggish boys in game themselves forswear,
          So the boy Love is perjured everywhere.
          For ere Demetrius looked on Hermia's eyne,
          He hailed down oaths that he was only mine.
          And when this hail some heat from Hermia felt,
          So he dissolved, and showers of oaths did melt.
          I will go tell him of fair Hermia's flight.
          Then to the wood will he tomorrow night   250
          Pursue her. And for this intelligence,
          If I have thanks, it is a dear expense.
          But herein mean I to enrich my pain,
          To have his sight thither, and back again.

                    Exit.

229. *o'or* – over

235. *holding no quantity* –
bearing no relation (to how
they are viewed by love)
237. *mind* – i.e., the
imagination
240. *figure* – symbolize

242. *beguiled* – deceived
243. "Just as mischievous
boys, in jest, will not keep
their word."
244. *is perjured* – does not
keep his word
245. *eyne* – eyes

251. *intelligence* – information

Act One
Scene 2

Athens. Quince's house.

A troupe of amateur actors meets at the home of Peter Quince, their director. They have decided to prepare an entertainment for the wedding festivities of Theseus and Hippolyta. Peter Quince assigns parts, and the actors agree to meet in the woods the following evening to rehearse their play.

2. *generally* – Bottom means "severally" or one at a time.
5. *interlude* – entertainment
11. *lamentable* – tragic
12. *Pyramus and Thisbe* – See the note about Shakespeare's sources on page 7 of the Introduction.

Pyramus and Thisbe

19. *tyrant* – in Elizabethan theatre, a stock character whose part involved ranting and overacting
23. *condole* – express grief
24. *humour* – inclination

25. *Ercles* – Hercules, a Greek hero of great strength and the son of Zeus. One of his many exploits involved killing a lion.

25 – 26. *make all split* – shatter everything, perhaps including eardrums

Enter Quince the Carpenter, and Snug the Joiner, and Bottom the Weaver, and Flute the Bellows-mender, and Snout the Tinker, and Starveling the Tailor.

QUINCE: Is all our company here?

BOTTOM: You were best to call them generally, man by man, according to the scrip.

QUINCE: Here is the scroll of every man's name, which is thought fit, through all Athens, to play in our interlude before the Duke and the Duchess, on his wedding-day at night.

Bottom: First, good Peter Quince, say what the play treats on; then read the names of the actors, and so grow to a point.   10

QUINCE: Marry, our play is The most lamentable comedy, and most cruel death of Pyramus and Thisbe.

BOTTOM: A very good piece of work, I assure you, and a merry. Now good Peter Quince, call forth your actors by the scroll. Masters, spread yourselves.

QUINCE: Answer as I call you. Nick Bottom, the weaver?

BOTTOM: Ready. Name what part I am for, and proceed.

QUINCE: You, Nick Bottom, are set down for Pyramus.

BOTTOM: What is Pyramus? A lover, or a tyrant?

QUINCE: A lover that kills himself most gallant for love.   20

BOTTOM: That will ask some tears in the true performing of it. If I do it, let the audience look to their eyes. I will move storms; I will condole in some measure. To the rest — yet, my chief humour is for a tyrant. I could play Ercles rarely, or a part to tear a cat in, to make all split.

The raging rocks,
And shivering shocks,
Shall break the locks
   Of prison gates;   30
And Phibbus' car
Shall shine from far,
And make and mar
   The foolish Fates.

This was lofty! Now name the rest of the players. This is Ercles' vein, a tyrant's vein. A lover is more condoling.

QUINCE: Francis Flute, the bellows-mender?

FLUTE: Here Peter Quince.

QUINCE: Flute, you must take Thisbe on you.

FLUTE: What is Thisbe? A wandering knight?   40

QUINCE: It is the lady that Pyramus must love.

FLUTE: Nay, faith, let me not play a woman. I have a beard coming.

QUINCE: That's all one. You shall play it in a mask, and you may speak as small as you will.

BOTTOM: And I may hide my face, let me play Thisbe too. I'll speak in a monstrous little voice, "Thisne, Thisne!" — "Ah, Pyramus, my lover dear! Thy Thisbe dear, and lady dear!"

QUINCE: No, no. You must play Pyramus and Flute, you   50 Thisbe.

BOTTOM: Well, proceed.

QUINCE: Robin Starveling, the tailor?

STARVELING: Here Peter Quince.

QUINCE: Robin Starveling, you must play Thisbe's mother. Tom Snout, the tinker?

SNOUT: Here Peter Quince.

QUINCE: You, Pyramus' father; myself, Thisbe's father; Snug, the joiner, you the lion's part. And, I hope, here is a play fitted.   60

SNUG: Have you the lion's part written? Pray you, if it be, give it me, for I am slow of study.

QUINCE: You may do it extempore, for it is nothing but roaring.

BOTTOM: Let me play the lion too. I will roar, that I will do any man's heart good to hear me. I will roar, that I will make the Duke say, "Let him roar again! Let him roar again!"

51620

---

31. *Phibbus' car* – the chariot of the sun god Phoebus Apollo, which he drove across the sky during the course of the day

Phibbus' car

34. *Fates* – the three goddesses who control human destiny

37. *Flute* – Shakespeare has chosen the names of the company with care. A bellows-mender repaired luted church organs. The name Flute also suggests the piping voice appropriate for one who will play a female part.

45. *small* – quietly but high-pitched

46. *And* – if

63. *extempore* – by improvising; ad lib

"[Their] names are not merely technical terms.... but also [terms] of things natural. 'Snout' has obvious animal connections ... The name 'Starveling' by its image of thinness brings in the body and food ... 'Snug' suggests a bodily, almost animal, warmth ... 'Quince' is fruit and tree. 'Flute' suggests ... the moving breath which is life itself ... Last and best, there is Bottom himself."
– Elizabeth Sewell, American scholar

75. *discretion* – choice
75. *aggravate* – to make worse or intensify. Bottom means to say the opposite "moderate." Many of Bottom's speeches contain *malapropisms*, words that sound similar to the intended words. The effect is often comical.

76. *sucking dove* – Bottom blends "sitting dove" with another common example of gentleness, the "sucking lamb."

86. *purple-in-grain* – red
87. *French-crown* – gold coin

QUINCE: If you should do it too terribly, you would fright the Duchess and the ladies, that they would shriek; and that were enough to hang us all.   70

ALL: That would hang us, every mother's son.

BOTTOM: I grant you, friends, if that you should fright the ladies out of their wits, they would have no more discretion but to hang us. But I will aggravate my voice so that I will roar you as gently as any sucking dove. I will roar you and 'twere any nightingale.

QUINCE: You can play no part but Pyramus, for Pyramus is a sweet-faced man, a proper man, as one shall see in a summer's day; a most lovely gentleman-like man. Therefore you must needs play Pyramus.   80

BOTTOM: Well, I will undertake it. What beard were I best to play it in?

QUINCE: Why? What you will.

BOTTOM: I will discharge it, in either your straw-colour beard, your orange-tawny beard, your purple-in-grain beard, or your French-crown-coloured beard, your perfect yellow.

QUINCE: Some of your French crowns have no hair at all, and then you will play bare-faced. But, masters, here are your parts, and I am to entreat you, request you, and desire you, to con them by tomorrow night; and meet me in the palace wood, a mile without the town, by moonlight. There will we rehearse, for if we meet in the city, we shall be dogged with company, and our devices known. In the meantime, I will draw a bill of properties, such as our play wants. I pray you, fail me not.

90

BOTTOM: We will meet, and there we may rehearse most obscenely, and courageously. Take pains, be perfect, adieu.

100

QUINCE: At the Duke's oak we meet.

BOTTOM: Enough. Hold or cut bow-strings.

Exeunt.

🐝 🐝 🐝

92. *con* – memorize

95. *devices* – plans
96. *bill of properties* – list of props

99. *obscenely* – Bottom perhaps means "unseen" or "obscurely" (hidden).
102. *Hold ... bow-strings* – The meaning of this line is unclear. According to some scholars, the expression may have a military origin. It offers the alternative of holding one's position or retreating. In a retreat, soldiers would cut their bow-strings to prevent the enemy from using their weapons.

Act One Considerations

ACT ONE Scene 1

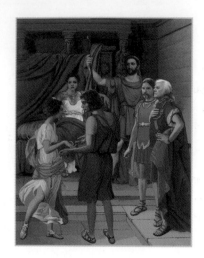

▶ Hippolyta speaks only five lines in this first scene. Why might Shakespeare have chosen to have her remain so silent? Create a dialogue between Theseus and Hippolyta that may have occurred after this scene.

▶ Write the law of Athens that Egeus invokes against his daughter, Hermia. Read your edict to the class.

▶ Debate or write a position paper on the following statement: Children who are not obedient to their parents' wishes—assuming that these wishes are reasonable and moral—should be punished by the law.

▶ A challenge for any director of this play is to distinguish between Demetrius and Lysander. If you were directing the play, how would you make these two lovers distinct?

▶ Imagine that you are designing the set for a stage version of this play. Create a sketch or describe in detail what the set would look like for this first scene. Explain your choices.

▶ Why does Helena decide to tell Demetrius of her friends' decision to leave Athens? What does this decision reveal about Helena's personality?

ACT ONE Scene 2

▶ All of the characters in this scene work in a trade. If you were modernizing this play, what changes would you make in their occupations? Make up new names for the characters to reflect their modern occupations. Explain the reasons for your changes.

▶ What are your first impressions of this amateur troupe of actors? Consider each actor individually. To what extent is Bottom the leader of this group? How does Quince exercise his leadership?

▶ A *malapropism* is a word that is used incorrectly by confusing it with a similar sounding word. Bottom is not the only character who misuses words. Find all the examples of malapropisms you can in this scene. Write three sentences from everyday conversation that contain a malapropism.

Act Two
Scene 1

A wood near Athens.

Enter a Fairy and [from the opposite direction] Puck.

PUCK: How now spirit, whither wander you?
FAIRY: Over hill, over dale,
        Thorough bush, thorough briar,
        Over park, over pale,
        Thorough flood, thorough fire,
        I do wander everywhere,
        Swifter than the moon's sphere;
        And I serve the Fairy Queen,
        To dew her orbs upon the green.
        The cowslips tall her pensioners be,   10
        In their gold coats spots you see;
        Those be rubies, fairy favours,
        In those freckles live their savours.
    I must go seek some dew-drops here
    And hang a pearl in every cowslip's ear.
    Farewell thou lob of spirits. I'll be gone.
    Our Queen and all her elves come here anon.
PUCK: The King doth keep his revels here tonight.
    Take heed the Queen come not within his sight,
    For Oberon is passing fell and wrath,   20
    Because that she, as her attendant, hath
    A lovely boy stolen from an Indian king,
    She never had so sweet a changeling,
    And jealous Oberon would have the child
    Knight of his train, to trace the forests wild.
    But she, perforce, withholds the loved boy,
    Crowns him with flowers, and makes him all her joy.
    And now they never meet in grove, or green,

Oberon, king of the fairies, has been quarrelling with Titania, queen of the fairies, over a changeling boy, whom she will not give up to him. Seeking to punish Titania, Oberon sends his servant Puck to get a magic flower. He plans to place its juice on Titania's eyelids so that when she awakens she will fall in love with the first living creature she sees. Then, overhearing Demetrius spurn Helena's love, Oberon orders Puck to apply the juice to Demetrius' eyes to force him to fall in love with Helena.

3. *thorough* – through
4. *park* – land protected by royal decree for game
4. *pale* – fence or land enclosed by a fence
9. *orbs* – circles; fairy rings
10. *pensioners* – royal bodyguards
12. *favours* – rewards, signs of royal approval
13. *savours* – perfumes
16. *lob* – oaf; clown
17. *anon* – soon
20. *passing ... wrath* – enraged
23. *changeling* – According to old tales, fairies took human children in the night and replaced them with fairy changelings, who were often deformed or weak. Here the term refers to the child taken away by fairies. See page 6 of the Introduction about belief in fairies.
25. *trace* – traverse; patrol
26. *perforce* – by force

By fountain clear, or spangled starlight sheen,
But they do square, that all their elves for fear   30
Creep into acorn cups, and hide them there.

FAIRY: Either I mistake your shape and making quite,
Or else you are that shrewd and knavish sprite
Called Robin Goodfellow. Are not you he,
That frights the maidens of the villagery,
Skim milk, and sometimes labour in the quern,
And bootless make the breathless housewife churn,
And sometime make the drink to bear no barm,
Mislead night-wanderers, laughing at their harm?
Those that Hobgoblin call you, and sweet Puck,   40
You do their work, and they shall have good luck.
Are not you he?

PUCK: Thou speakest aright;
I am that merry wanderer of the night.
I jest to Oberon and make him smile
When I a fat and bean-fed horse beguile,
Neighing in likeness of a filly foal,
And sometime lurk I in a gossip's bowl,
In very likeness of a roasted crab,
And when she drinks, against her lips I bob,   50
And on her withered dewlap pour the ale.
The wisest aunt, telling the saddest tale,
Sometime for three-foot stool mistaketh me,
Then slip I from her bum, down topples she,
And "tailor" cries, and falls into a cough.
And then the whole quire hold their hips, and laugh,
And waxen in their mirth, and neeze, and swear
A merrier hour was never wasted there.
But room fairy, here comes Oberon.

FAIRY: And here, my mistress. Would that he were gone!   60

Enter Oberon, the King of Fairies, [from one direction]
with his train; and Titania, the Queen,
[from another direction] with hers.

OBERON: Ill met by moonlight, proud Titania.

TITANIA: What, jealous Oberon? Fairies, skip hence.
I have forsworn his bed and company.

OBERON: Tarry, rash wanton. Am not I thy lord?

TITANIA: Then I must be thy lady, but I know
When thou hast stolen away from fairy land,
And in the shape of Corin, sat all day,
Playing on pipes of corn and versing love

---

29. *spangled ... sheen* – bright, sparkling starlight
30. *square* – argue; squabble
32. *making* – form; appearance
34. *Robin Goodfellow* – Fairy stories of this merry prankster date back to the thirteenth century. If left cream to eat, he swept the house and performed other chores. If left no treat, he played cruel tricks on the householder.
36 – 39. Robin's pranks included taking the cream from milk, so that domestic workers could not churn it into butter; stopping fermentation in the making of beer or wine by neutralizing the yeast (*barm*); and disorienting night wanderers.
40. *Hobgoblin* – Shakespeare was the first to associate Robin Goodfellow with Hobgoblin.
46. *beguile* – deceive
49. *crab* – crab apple
51. *dewlap* – loose fold of skin around the throat. The term is most often used with cattle.
55. *tailor* – in Shakespeare's day, a cry commonly made upon falling on one's "tail"
56. *quire* – choir; company
57. *waxen* – increase
57. *neeze* – sneeze

RELATED READING

Robin Goodfellow – drama
by Aurand Harris (page 108)

63. *forsworn* – vowed to avoid
64. *Tarry, rash wanton* – "Wait, you hasty, undisciplined person."

To amorous Phillida. Why art thou here
Come from the farthest steppe of India, 70
But that, forsooth, the bouncing Amazon,
Your buskined mistress, and your warrior love,
To Theseus must be wedded, and you come
To give their bed joy and prosperity.

OBERON: How canst thou thus, for shame, Titania,
Glance at my credit with Hippolyta,
Knowing I know thy love to Theseus?
Didst thou not lead him through the glimmering night
From Perigenia, whom he ravished?
And make him with fair Aegles break his faith 80
With Ariadne, and Antiopa?

TITANIA: These are the forgeries of jealousy.
And never, since the middle summer's spring,
Met we on hill, in dale, forest, or mead,
By paved fountain, or by rushy brook,
Or in the beached margent of the sea,
To dance our ringlets to the whistling wind,
But with thy brawls thou hast disturbed our sport.
Therefore the winds, piping to us in vain,
As in revenge, have sucked up from the sea 90
Contagious fogs. Which, falling in the land,
Have every pelting river made so proud
That they have overborne their continents.
The ox hath therefore stretched his yoke in vain,
The ploughman lost his sweat, and the green corn
Hath rotted, ere his youth attained a beard.
The fold stands empty in the drowned field,
And crows are fatted with the murrion flock.
The nine men's morris is filled up with mud,
And the quaint mazes in the wanton green, 100
For lack of tread, are undistinguishable.
The human mortals want their winter cheer.
No night is now with hymn or carol blest.
Therefore the moon, the governess of floods,
Pale in her anger, washes all the air,
That rheumatic diseases do abound.
And, thorough this distemperature, we see
The seasons alter. Hoary-headed frosts
Fall in the fresh lap of the crimson rose,
And on old Hiems' thin and icy crown, 110
An odorous chaplet of sweet summer buds
Is, as in mockery, set. The spring, the summer,
The childing autumn, angry winter change

67 – 69. *Corin ... Phillida* –
common names in literature for
a shepherd and shepherdess
71. *forsooth* – truly
72. *buskined* – wearing high
leather boots

buskins

76. *Glance ... credit* – speak
mockingly of my reputation
79 – 81. *Perigenia, Aegles,
Ariadne, Antiopa* – women
whom Theseus abandoned or
betrayed in the course of his
travels and adventures before
the events of this play
82. *forgeries* – lies
83. *middle ... spring* –
beginning of midsummer
85. *rushy* – fringed with rushes
86. *margent* – margin; edge
87. *ringlets* – circular dances
91. *contagious* – noxious
92. *pelting* – petty
93. *overborne ... continents* –
caused extensive flooding
95. *lost his sweat* – worked in
vain
98. *murrion* – diseased
99. *nine men's morris* – rustic
dance which involves a
chesslike element
102. *want* – lack
106. *That* – so that

110. *Hiems* – god of winter
111. *chaplet* – wreath
113. *childing* – fruitful

114. *wonted liveries* – customary appearance
114. *mazed* – confused; amazed
115. *By ... increase* – what they bring forth
116. *progeny* – offspring

"In contemporary productions ... it is common practice to double the parts of the human rulers, Duke Theseus and his bride Hippolyta, with the king and queen of the fairy world, Oberon and Titania. Maybe there is some saving in salaries this way."
– Molly Maureen Mahood, British scholar and professor

122. *henchman* – page
125. *votress* – worshipper who has taken sacred vows
128. *Neptune* – Roman god of the sea
130. *conceive* – fill with wind so as to resemble a pregnant woman
131. *wanton* – playful

"Shakespeare's romantic comedies begin with feuding, misunderstandings, and obstacles and end with dancing, music, and marriage. To the Elizabethans, song and dance were symbols of cosmic harmony."
– Norrie Epstein, American author

144. *spare* – avoid
147. *chide* – quarrel
151. *Since* – the time when

Their wonted liveries, and the mazed world,
By their increase, now knows not which is which.
And this same progeny of evils,
Comes from our debate, from our dissension.
We are their parents and original.

OBERON: Do you amend it then. It lies in you.
Why should Titania cross her Oberon?   120
I do but beg a little changeling boy,
To be my henchman.

TITANIA: Set your heart at rest.
The fairy land buys not the child of me.
His mother was a votress of my order,
And in the spiced Indian air, by night,
Full often hath she gossiped by my side,
And sat with me on Neptune's yellow sands,
Marking the embarked traders on the flood,
When we have laughed to see the sails conceive,   130
And grow big-bellied with the wanton wind;
Which she, with pretty and with swimming gait,
Following, her womb then rich with my young squire,
Would imitate, and sail upon the land,
To fetch me trifles, and return again,
As from a voyage, rich with merchandise.
But she, being mortal, of that boy did die,
And for her sake do I rear up her boy,
And for her sake I will not part with him.

OBERON: How long within this wood intend you stay?   140

TITANIA: Perchance till after Theseus' wedding-day.
If you will patiently dance in our round,
And see our moonlight revels, go with us.
If not, shun me, and I will spare your haunts.

OBERON: Give me that boy, and I will go with thee.

TITANIA: Not for thy fairy kingdom. Fairies away.
We shall chide downright, if I longer stay.

Exeunt Titania with her train.

OBERON: Well, go thy way. Thou shalt not from this grove
Till I torment thee for this injury.
My gentle Puck, come hither. Thou rememb'rest   150
Since once I sat upon a promontory,
And heard a mermaid, on a dolphin's back,
Uttering such dulcet and harmonious breath,
That the rude sea grew civil at her song,
And certain stars shot madly from their spheres,
To hear the sea-maid's music.

PUCK: I remember.

OBERON: That very time I saw, but thou couldst not,
    Flying between the cold moon and the earth,
    Cupid all armed. A certain aim he took   160
    At a fair vestal, throned by the west,
    And loosed his love-shaft smartly from his bow,
    As it should pierce a hundred thousand hearts.
    But I might see young Cupid's fiery shaft
    Quenched in the chaste beams of the watery moon,
    And the imperial votress passed on,
    In maiden meditation, fancy-free.
    Yet marked I where the bolt of Cupid fell.
    It fell upon a little western flower,
    Before, milk-white, now purple with love's wound,   170
    And maidens call it, "love-in-idleness."
    Fetch me that flower. The herb I showed thee once,
    The juice of it, on sleeping eye-lids laid,
    Will make or man or woman madly dote
    Upon the next live creature that it sees.
    Fetch me this herb, and be thou here again,
    Ere the leviathan can swim a league.

PUCK: I'll put a girdle round about the earth
    In forty minutes.

[Exit Puck.]

OBERON: Having once this juice,   180
    I'll watch Titania, when she is asleep,
    And drop the liquor of it in her eyes.
    The next thing then she, waking, looks upon,
    Be it on lion, bear, or wolf, or bull,
    On meddling monkey, or on busy ape,
    She shall pursue it, with the soul of love.
    And ere I take this charm from off her sight,
    As I can take it with another herb,
    I'll make her render up her page to me.
    But who comes here? I am invisible,   190
    And I will overhear their conference.

Enter Demetrius, Helena following him.

DEMETRIUS: I love thee not, therefore pursue me not.
    Where is Lysander, and fair Hermia?
    The one I'll slay, the other slayeth me.
    Thou told'st me they were stolen unto this wood;
    And here am I, and wood, within this wood,

161. Many scholars believe that this is a veiled compliment to Queen Elizabeth I, who was known as the Virgin *(vestal)* Queen.

162. *love-shaft* – arrow
164. *might* – was able to
165 – 66. It was believed that the magic power of Cupid's arrow was neutralized by moonbeams. Diana, the goddess of hunting and chastity, was also associated with the moon.
171. *love-in-idleness* – pansies
174. *or ... or* – either ... or
177. *leviathan* – whale
178 *put a girdle* – circle

178 – 79. In 1957, Puck's feat was almost equalled. Russia launched Sputnik, which circled the globe in 47 minutes.

"In Athens we heard that Theseus has won Hippolyta's love 'doing [her] injuries,' and we saw Egeus, Demetrius, and the law combine in an effort to win Hermia's love doing her injuries, and now we see Oberon trying to win Titania's love doing *her* injuries."
– James L. Calderwood (b. 1930), American professor, University of California

190. *I am invisible* – Oberon's cue to the audience that he will remain on stage and not be seen by the others

196. *wood* – triple level of pun: woed (woeful), wood (insane), woo'd (being wooed)

Act Two • Scene 1

201. *Leave you* – give up

210. *leave* – permission
216. *sick* – nauseated
217. *sick* – not well
218. "You risk damaging your virtuous reputation"
224. *privilege* – protection

231. *brakes* – bushes
235 – 37. Helena compares her plight to the reversal of several familiar chase sequences taken from mythology and nature. The Roman poet Ovid tells the story of Apollo, who fell in love with and relentlessly pursued Daphne. As she fled from his advances, she desperately prayed for help and was rescued when the gods transformed her into a laurel tree. Another Greek myth tells of the griffin, a ferocious mythical beast with the body of a lion and the head and wings of an eagle. The *hind* is a female deer, a common prey of the tiger.

griffin

237. *Bootless* – useless
239. *stay* – wait to hear
239. *questions* – arguments

Because I cannot meet my Hermia.
Hence, get thee gone, and follow me no more.
HELENA: You draw me, you hard-hearted adamant,
But yet you draw not iron, for my heart   200
Is true as steel. Leave you your power to draw,
And I shall have no power to follow you.
DEMETRIUS: Do I entice you? Do I speak you fair?
Or rather do I not in plainest truth,
Tell you I do not, nor I cannot love you?
HELENA: And even for that do I love you the more.
I am your spaniel, and Demetrius,
The more you beat me, I will fawn on you.
Use me but as your spaniel: spurn me, strike me,
Neglect me, lose me. Only give me leave,   210
Unworthy as I am, to follow you.
What worser place can I beg in your love,
And yet a place of high respect with me,
Than to be used as you use your dog?
DEMETRIUS: Tempt not too much the hatred of my spirit,
For I am sick when I do look on thee.
HELENA: And I am sick when I look not on you.
DEMETRIUS: You do impeach your modesty too much,
To leave the city, and commit yourself
Into the hands of one that loves you not,   220
To trust the opportunity of night
And the ill counsel of a desert place
With the rich worth of your virginity.
HELENA: Your virtue is my privilege. For that
It is not night when I do see your face,
Therefore I think I am not in the night.
Nor doth this wood lack worlds of company,
For you, in my respect, are all the world.
Then how can it be said I am alone,
When all the world is here to look on me?   230
DEMETRIUS: I'll run from thee, and hide me in the brakes,
And leave thee to the mercy of wild beasts.
HELENA: The wildest hath not such a heart as you.
Run when you will, the story shall be changed:
Apollo flies, and Daphne holds the chase;
The dove pursues the griffin; the mild hind
Makes speed to catch the tiger. Bootless speed,
When cowardice pursues, and valour flies.
DEMETRIUS: I will not stay thy questions. Let me go,
Or if thou follow me, do not believe,   240
But I shall do thee mischief in the wood.

HELENA: Ay, in the temple, in the town, the field,
  You do me mischief. Fie Demetrius,
  Your wrongs do set a scandal on my sex.
  We cannot fight for love, as men may do.
  We should be woo'd and were not made to woo.

[Exit Demetrius.]

  I'll follow thee and make a heaven of hell,
  To die upon the hand I love so well.

Exit [Helena].

OBERON: Fare thee well, nymph. Ere he do leave this grove,
  Thou shalt fly him, and he shall seek thy love.   250

Enter Puck.

  Hast thou the flower there? Welcome, wanderer.
PUCK: Ay, there it is.
OBERON: I pray thee give it me.
  I know a bank where the wild thyme blows,
  Where oxlips and the nodding violet grows,
  Quite over-canopied with luscious woodbine,
  With sweet musk-roses, and with eglantine.
  There sleeps Titania, sometime of the night,
  Lulled in these flowers, with dances and delight;
  And there the snake throws her enamelled skin,   260
  Weed wide enough to wrap a fairy in,
  And with the juice of this I'll streak her eyes,
  And make her full of hateful fantasies.
  Take thou some of it, and seek through this grove.
  A sweet Athenian lady is in love
  With a disdainful youth. Anoint his eyes,
  But do it when the next thing he espies
  May be the lady. Thou shalt know the man,
  By the Athenian garments he hath on.
  Effect it with some care, that he may prove   270
  More fond on her than she upon her love.
  And look thou meet me ere the first cock crow.
PUCK: Fear not my lord, your servant shall do so.

Exeunt.

244. *scandal* – mockery
249. *nymph* – young woman
250. *fly* – flee from

RELATED READINGS

Midsummer Night Flowers – poem by Nimmi Rashid (page 112)

I Cannot See What Flowers Are at My Feet – poem by John Keats (page 114)

255. *oxlips* – flowering plants
256. *woodbine* – honeysuckle

woodbine

257. *eglantine* – a variety of wild rose

eglantine

260. *throws* – discards
261. *Weed* – clothing
263. *hateful fantasies* – disgusting delusions
267. *espies* – looks upon
271. "More in love with her than she is with him."

Once Titania has been sung to sleep, Oberon applies the love potion to her eyes. Hermia and Lysander, exhausted because they have been wandering through the forest all night, also fall asleep. Puck mistakes Lysander for Demetrius and applies the love potion to his eyes. Helena wakens Lysander, and he falls instantly in love with her. Believing that Lysander is mocking her, Helena runs away. Hermia wakes to find that Lysander has disappeared.

1. *roundel* – dance performed in a circle
3. *cankers* – tiny worms; caterpillars
4. *rere-mice* – bats
7. *quaint* – dainty

13. *Philomel* – the nightingale

Philomel

17. *nigh* – near

Act Two
Scene 2

Another part of the wood.

Enter Titania, Queen of the Fairies, with her train.

TITANIA: Come, now a roundel, and a fairy song.
　　　　　Then, for the third part of a minute, hence:
　　　　　Some to kill cankers in the musk-rose buds,
　　　　　Some war with rere-mice for their leathern wings,
　　　　　To make my small elves coats, and some keep back
　　　　　The clamorous owl, that nightly hoots and wonders
　　　　　At our quaint spirits. Sing me now asleep;
　　　　　Then to your offices, and let me rest.

The Fairies sing.

FAIRIES: *You spotted snakes with double tongue,*
　　　　　Thorny hedgehogs be not seen,　　　　　　　　　10
　　　　　Newts and blind-worms, do no wrong,
　　　　　Come not near our Fairy Queen.
　　　　　　　Philomel, with melody
　　　　　　　Sing in our sweet lullaby,
　　　　Lulla, lulla, lullaby, lulla, lulla, lullaby,
　　　　　　　Never harm, nor spell, nor charm,
　　　　　　　Come our lovely lady nigh,
　　　　　　　So good night, with lullaby.
1. FAIRY: *Weaving spiders come not here,*
　　　　　Hence you long-legged spinners, hence!　　　　20
　　　　　Beetles black approach not near;
　　　　　Worm nor snail do no offence.
　　　　　　　Philomel, with melody, etc.

2. FAIRY: Hence, away! Now all is well:
One aloof, stand sentinel.

Titania sleeps. [Exeunt Fairies.]
Enter Oberon [and squeezes juice of the flower
on Titania's eyelids].

OBERON: What thou seest, when thou dost wake,
Do it for thy true-love take.
Love and languish for his sake.
Be it ounce, or cat, or bear,
Pard, or boar with bristled hair,   30
In thy eye that shall appear,
When thou wak'st, it is thy dear.
Wake when some vile thing is near.

[Exit Oberon.]
Enter Lysander and Hermia.

LYSANDER: Fair love, you faint with wand'ring in the wood,
And to speak troth, I have forgot our way.
We'll rest us Hermia, if you think it good,
And tarry for the comfort of the day.
HERMIA: Be it so Lysander. Find you out a bed,
For I upon this bank will rest my head.
LYSANDER: One turf shall serve as pillow for us both,   40
One heart, one bed, two bosoms, and one troth.
HERMIA: Nay good Lysander, for my sake, my dear
Lie further off yet, do not lie so near.
LYSANDER: O take the sense, sweet, of my innocence!
Love takes the meaning, in love's conference.
I mean that my heart unto yours is knit,
So that but one heart we can make of it.
Two bosoms interchained with an oath,
So then two bosoms, and a single troth.
Then by your side, no bed-room me deny,   50
For lying so, Hermia, I do not lie.
HERMIA: Lysander riddles very prettily.
Now much beshrew my manners and my pride,
If Hermia meant to say, Lysander lied.
But gentle friend, for love and courtesy,
Lie further off, in human modesty.
Such separation as may well be said
Becomes a virtuous bachelor, and a maid,
So far be distant, and good night sweet friend.
Thy love ne'er alter till thy sweet life end!   60

25. *aloof* – apart; at a distance

29. *ounce* – lynx
30. *Pard* – leopard

35. *troth* – truth
37. *tarry* – wait

"To be lost in the forest is to be lost to *this* world, to be abandoned by the light, to lose yourself utterly with no guarantee you will either find yourself or else be found."
  Angela Carter (b. 1940), English novelist

45. "Love enables true lovers to understand each other."
49. *troth* – true love

53. *beshrew* – condemn; curse (in a mild sense)

60. *ne'er* – never

LYSANDER: Amen, amen, to that fair prayer, say I,
And then end life, when I end loyalty.
Here is my bed, sleep give thee all his rest.
HERMIA: With half that wish, the wisher's eyes be pressed!

They sleep.
Enter Puck.

PUCK: Through the forest have I gone,
But Athenian found I none,
On whose eyes I might approve
This flower's force in stirring love.
Night and silence! Who is here?
Weeds of Athens he doth wear.   70
This is he, my master said,
Despised the Athenian maid,
And here the maiden sleeping sound,
On the dank and dirty ground.
Pretty soul, she durst not lie
Near this lack-love, this kill-courtesy.
Churl, upon thy eyes I throw
All the power this charm doth owe.
When thou wak'st, let love forbid
Sleep his seat on thy eyelid.   80
So awake when I am gone,
For I must now to Oberon.

67. *approve* – test

70. *Weeds* – clothing

75. *durst* – dares
77. *Churl* – brutish, insensitive fellow
78. *owe* – own

Exit.
Enter Demetrius and Helena running.

HELENA: Stay, though thou kill me, sweet Demetrius.
DEMETRIUS: I charge thee hence, and do not haunt me thus.
HELENA: O, wilt thou darkling leave me? Do not so.   85. *darkling* – in the dark
DEMETRIUS: Stay, on thy peril; I alone will go.

Exit Demetrius.

HELENA: O, I am out of breath, in this fond chase.   87. *fond* – foolish
    The more my prayer, the lesser is my grace.
    Happy is Hermia, wheresoever she lies,
    For she hath blessed and attractive eyes.   90
    How came her eyes so bright? Not with salt tears.
    If so, my eyes are oftener washed than hers.
    No, no. I am as ugly as a bear!
    For beasts that meet me, run away for fear,
    Therefore no marvel, though Demetrius
    Do, as a monster, fly my presence thus.
    What wicked and dissembling glass of mine
    Made me compare with Hermia's sphery eyne?   98. *sphery* – bright (as the
    But who is here? Lysander, on the ground!   stars)
    Dead, or asleep? I see no blood, no wound.   100
    Lysander, if you live, good sir awake.

LYSANDER: *[Waking.]*
And run through fire I will for thy sweet sake.
Transparent Helena! Nature shows art,
That through thy bosom makes me see thy heart.
Where is Demetrius? Oh how fit a word
Is that vile name, to perish on my sword!

HELENA: Do not say so, Lysander, say not so.
What though he love your Hermia? Lord, what though?
Yet Hermia still loves you. Then be content.

LYSANDER: Content with Hermia? No, I do repent   110
The tedious minutes I with her have spent.
Not Hermia, but Helena I love.
Who will not change a raven for a dove?
The will of man is by his reason swayed,
And reason says you are the worthier maid.
Things growing are not ripe until their season.
So I, being young, till now ripe not to reason,
And touching now the point of human skill,
Reason becomes the marshal to my will,
And leads me to your eyes, where I o'erlook   120
Love's stories, written in love's richest book.

HELENA: Wherefore was I to this keen mockery born?
When at your hands did I deserve this scorn?
Is't not enough, is't not enough, young man,
That I did never, no nor never can,
Deserve a sweet look from Demetrius' eye,
But you must flout my insufficiency?
Good troth you do me wrong, good sooth you do,
In such disdainful manner, me to woo.
But fare you well. Perforce I must confess,   130
I thought you lord of more true gentleness.
O, that a lady of one man refused,
Should of another therefore be abused!

Exit Helena.

LYSANDER: She sees not Hermia. Hermia sleep thou there,
And never mayst thou come Lysander near,
For as a surfeit of the sweetest things
The deepest loathing to the stomach brings;
Or as the heresies that men do leave
Are hated most of those they did deceive,
So thou, my surfeit, and my heresy,   140
Of all be hated, but the most of me!
And all my powers address your love and might
To honour Helen, and to be her knight.

Exit Lysander.

HERMIA: *[Waking, startled.]*
    Help me Lysander, help me! Do thy best
    To pluck this crawling serpent from my breast!
    Ay me, for pity. What a dream was here?
    Lysander look, how I do quake with fear.
    Methought a serpent ate my heart away,
    And you sat smiling at his cruel prey.
    Lysander! What, removed? Lysander! Lord!   150   150. *removed* – moved away
    What, out of hearing? Gone? No sound, no word?
    Alack where are you? Speak, and if you hear,
    Speak, of all loves! I swoon almost with fear.
    No? Then I well perceive you are not nigh.
    Either death or you I'll find immediately.

                    Exit.

            ❧   ❧   ❧

Act Two Considerations

ACT TWO Scene 1

▶ Research any of the myths associated with Perigenia, Aegles, Ariadne, and Antiopa, women whom Theseus betrayed before the events of this play, and retell the story in your own words. On the basis of your findings, what conclusions can you draw about the character of mythological Theseus?

▶ Many of our present-day beliefs about fairies come from Shakespeare's portrayal of fairies in his plays. What are the basic characteristics of fairies as presented in *A Midsummer Night's Dream*? How do these characteristics compare with our present-day beliefs?

▶ The Elizabethans believed that when the natural order of the universe was disrupted, nature reflected that disorder through events such as those described by Titania in lines 82 to 118. What specific aspects of the natural order are violated through Titania's decision to keep the changeling boy? Rewrite this speech using modern-day language.

▶ The scene between Demetrius and Helena greatly depends on physical action. Shakespeare does not provide any stage directions to indicate how the scene should be played. Create a series of stage directions that describe how this scene would unfold if you were directing the play.

▶ Although Oberon is a fairyland king, he has many human characteristics. Make a list of his human character traits that are revealed in this scene. For each trait, provide evidence from the scene that supports its attribution to Oberon.

▶ As Oberon places the potion on Titania's eyes, he wishes that his wife will wake "when some vile thing is near." Of all the characters introduced so far in this play, with whom do you think Shakespeare will have Titania fall in love? Explain.

▶ Under the influence of the love-potion, Lysander attempts to explain his love for Helena (lines 114 to 121). Paraphrase in your own words Lysander's speech. Why is this speech ironic?

▶ Hermia, upon waking, describes the first of many dreams in this play. In what ways is this dream more than a dream?

Act Three
Scene 1

The wood.

Deep in the forest outside Athens' gates, the amateur actors meet as promised to rehearse their play. Puck places an ass's head on Bottom, and the company of actors flee in horror. Titania awakes and falls in love with the transformed Bottom. She instructs her fairies to attend to Bottom's every need and wish.

Titania lying asleep.
Enter Quince, Snug, Bottom, Flute, Snout,
and Starveling.

BOTTOM: Are we all met?

QUINCE: Pat, pat; and here's a marvellous convenient place for our rehearsal. This green plot shall be our stage, this hawthorn-brake our tiring-house; and we will do it in action as we will do it before the Duke.

BOTTOM: Peter Quince?

QUINCE: What sayest thou, bully Bottom?

BOTTOM: There are things in this comedy of Pyramus and Thisbe that will never please. First, Pyramus must draw a sword to kill himself; which the ladies cannot abide.   10
How answer you that?

SNOUT: By'r lakin, a parlous fear.

STARVELING: I believe we must leave the killing out, when all is done.

BOTTOM: Not a whit. I have a device to make all well. Write me a prologue, and let the prologue seem to say, we will do no harm with our swords, and that Pyramus is not killed indeed. And, for the more better assurance, tell them that I, Pyramus am not Pyramus, but Bottom the weaver. This will put them out of fear.   20

QUINCE: Well, we will have such a prologue, and it shall be written in eight and six.

BOTTOM: No, make it two more. Let it be written in eight and eight.

SNOUT: Will not the ladies be afeard of the lion?

STARVELING: I fear it, I promise you.

2. *Pat, pat* – right on time

4. *tiring-house* – dressing room and area where actors wait for their cue

7. *bully* – good friend

10. *abide* – endure

12. "By our Lady, a terrible fear."

RELATED READING

A Fragment of Manuscript – science fiction by Harry Harrison (page 116)

22. *eight and six* – The typical metre for ballads consisted of alternating lines of eight and six syllables.

BOTTOM: Masters, you ought to consider with yourself. To bring in, God shield us, a lion among ladies, is a most dreadful thing. For there is not a more fearful wild-fowl than your lion living, and we ought to look to it.   30

SNOUT: Therefore, another prologue must tell he is not a lion.

BOTTOM: Nay, you must name his name, and half his face must be seen through the lion's neck, and he himself must speak through, saying thus, or to the same defect, "Ladies," or "Fair ladies, I would wish you," or "I would request you," or "I would entreat you, not to fear, not to tremble. My life for yours. If you think I come hither as a lion, it were pity of my life. No, I am no such thing. I am a man as other men are," and there indeed,   40 let him name his name, and tell them plainly he is Snug the joiner.

QUINCE: Well, it shall be so. But there is two hard things: that is, to bring the moonlight into a chamber; for you know, Pyramus and Thisbe meet by moonlight.

SNOUT: Doth the moon shine that night we play our play?

BOTTOM: A calendar, a calendar! Look in the almanac! Find out moonshine, find out moonshine.

QUINCE: Yes, it doth shine that night.

BOTTOM: Why then may you leave a casement of the great   50 chamber window, where we play, open, and the moon may shine in at the casement.

QUINCE: Ay, or else one must come in with a bush of thorns and a lantern, and say he comes to disfigure, or to present the person of Moonshine. Then, there is another thing. We must have a wall in the great chamber, for Pyramus and Thisbe, says the story, did talk through the chink of a wall.

SNOUT: You can never bring in a wall. What say you, Bottom?   60

BOTTOM: Some man or other must present Wall, and let him have some plaster, or some loam, or some rough-cast about him, to signify wall; and let him hold his fingers thus, and through that cranny shall Pyramus and Thisbe whisper.

QUINCE: If that may be, then all is well. Come, sit down every mother's son, and rehearse your parts. Pyramus, you begin. When you have spoken your speech, enter into that brake, and so every one according to his cue.

Enter Puck [from behind].

Notes:

29. *wild-fowl* – Bottom means to say "beast," but "fowl" is more alliterative in this line. See quote by G.K. Chesterton on page 47.

35. *defect* – Bottom means "effect" but says "defect."

50. *casement* – window

53 – 55. The story of the man in the moon and why he should have a bush of thorns has a distinct origin. According to J. Brand in *Observations on the Popular Antiquities of Great Britain* (1849), an "'ancient and popular superstition' tells of a 'poor man which stole a bundle of thorns' for firewood, and was punished by being 'set into the moon, there for to abide for ever.'"

58. *chink* – crack; hole

PUCK: What hempen home-spuns have we swaggering here, 70
    So near the cradle of the fairy queen?
    What, a play toward! I'll be an auditor;
    An actor too perhaps, if I see cause.
QUINCE: Speak, Pyramus. Thisbe, stand forth.
BOTTOM: *Thisbe, the flowers of odious savours sweet,—*
QUINCE: Odorous, odorous!
BOTTOM: *— odorous savours sweet,*
    So hath thy breath, my dearest Thisbe dear.
    But hark, a voice! Stay thou but here awhile,
    And by and by I will to thee appear. 80

Exit [Bottom, behind a bush].

PUCK: A stranger Pyramus than ever played here.

[Exit Puck, following Bottom.]

FLUTE: Must I speak now?
QUINCE: Ay, marry, must you. For you must understand he goes but to see a noise that he heard, and is to come again.
FLUTE: *Most radiant Pyramus, most lily-white of hue,*
    Of colour like the red rose, on triumphant briar,
    Most brisky juvenal and eke most lovely Jew,
    As true as truest horse, that yet would never tire,
    I'll meet thee, Pyramus, at Ninny's tomb. 90
QUINCE: "Ninus' tomb," man. Why, you must not speak that yet. That you answer to Pyramus. You speak all your part at once, cues and all. Pyramus enter. Your cue is past. It is, "never tire."
FLUTE: O — *As true as truest horse, that yet would never tire.*

[Enter Puck, and Bottom with an ass's head.]

BOTTOM: *If I were fair, Thisbe, I were only thine.*
QUINCE: O monstrous! O strange! We are haunted! Pray, masters! Fly, masters! Help!

[Exeunt running, Quince, Snug, Flute, Snout, and Starveling.]

PUCK: I'll follow you! I'll lead you about a round,
    Through bog, through bush, through brake, through briar: 100
    Sometime a horse I'll be, sometime a hound,

70. *hempen home-spuns* – coarsely dressed clowns or oafs
72. *auditor* – listener

"Bottom's literary taste is almost everywhere concerned with sound rather than sense. He begins the rehearsal with a boisterous readiness, 'Thisbe, the flowers of odious savours sweet.' Bottom's version is an immeasurably finer and more resonant line. The 'i' which he inserts [in odorous] is an inspiration of metricism."
G.K. Chesterton (1874–1936), British novelist, poet, and essayist

75. *odious* – foul smelling
76. *odorous* – sweet smelling
88. *brisky juvenal* – lively juvenile
88. *eke* – also
88. *Jew* – possibly a shortened form of *juvenile* to rhyme with *hue*
90. *Ninny* – fool
91. *Ninus* – a king of Nineveh

A hog, a headless bear, sometime a fire,
And neigh, and bark, and grunt, and roar, and burn,
Like horse, hound, hog, bear, fire, at every turn.

Exit [Puck].

BOTTOM: Why do they run away? This is a knavery of them
to make me afeard.

Enter Snout.

SNOUT: O Bottom, thou art changed! What do I see on thee?
BOTTOM: What do you see? You see an asshead of your own,
do you?

[Exit running, Snout.]
Enter Quince.

QUINCE: Bless thee Bottom, bless thee! Thou art translated.   110

Exit [running, Quince].

BOTTOM: I see their knavery. This is to make an ass of me,
to fright me, if they could. But I will not stir from this
place, do what they can. I will walk up and down here,
and I will sing, that they shall hear I am not afraid.

[Sings.]

The ousel cock, so black of hue,
With orange-tawny bill,
The throstle, with his note so true,
The wren, with little quill,—

TITANIA: *[Awaking because of the singing.]*
What angel wakes me from my flowery bed?
BOTTOM: *[Sings.]*
The finch, the sparrow, and the lark,   120
The plain-song cuckoo gray,
Whose note, full many a man doth mark,
And dares not answer, nay—

For, indeed, who would set his wit to so foolish a bird?
Who would give a bird the lie, though he cry "cuckoo"
never so?

105. *knavery* – treachery

108. Bottom is not aware
that he now bears an ass's
head. His lines are ironic.

110. *translated* – transformed

115. *ousel cock* – male
blackbird
117. *throstle* – thrush

124. *set his wit to* – argue
with
126. *never so* – ever so much

TITANIA: I pray thee, gentle mortal, sing again.
Mine ear is much enamoured of thy note.
So is mine eye enthralled to thy shape,
And thy fair virtue's force, perforce, doth move me,   130
On the first view to say, to swear, I love thee.

BOTTOM: Methinks mistress, you should have little reason
for that. And yet, to say the truth, reason and love keep
little company together, now-a-days. The more the pity,
that some honest neighbours will not make them friends.
Nay, I can gleek upon occasion.

TITANIA: Thou art as wise as thou art beautiful.

BOTTOM: Not so, neither. But if I had wit enough to get out
of this wood, I have enough to serve mine own turn.

TITANIA: Out of this wood do not desire to go.   140
Thou shalt remain here, whether thou wilt or no.
I am a spirit of no common rate.
The summer still doth tend upon my state,
And I do love thee. Therefore, go with me.
I'll give thee fairies to attend on thee,
And they shall fetch thee jewels from the deep,
And sing, while thou on pressed flowers, dost sleep.
And I will purge thy mortal grossness so,
That thou shalt like an airy spirit go.
Peaseblossom, Cobweb, Moth, and Mustardseed!   150

Enter Peaseblossom, Cobweb, Moth, and Mustardseed.

PEASEBLOSSOM: Ready.
COBWEB: And I.
MOTH: And I.
MUSTARDSEED: And I.
ALL: Where shall we go?
TITANIA: Be kind and courteous to this gentleman,
Hop in his walks, and gambol in his eyes,
Feed him with apricocks, and dewberries,
With purple grapes, green figs, and mulberries;
The honey-bags steal from the humble-bees,   160
And for night-tapers, crop their waxen thighs,
And light them at the fiery glow-worm's eyes,
To have my love to bed, and to arise;
And pluck the wings from painted butterflies,
To fan the moonbeams from his sleeping eyes.
Nod to him, elves, and do him courtesies.

136. *gleek* – make a joke
142. *rate* – rank
143. *still doth tend* – always attends or depends. Titania's power controls the seasons.
148 – 49. Titania offers to make Bottom an immortal like herself.
150. *Peaseblossom* – the delicate flower of the pea plant

peaseblossom

157. "Hop where he walks, and dance in front of his eyes"
160. *humble-bees* – bumble-bees
161. *night-tapers* – candles

"*A Midsummer Night's Dream* is one of the most magical plays ever written. It is a story of flowers and young lovers and dreams, and of the fairies who lived in an enchanted wood near Athens in the days when Theseus came back a conqueror. Most of it is played by moonlight, and anyone who has been outdoors on a moonlit night knows how changed and how lovely the world can be."
– Marchette Chute (b. 1909), American literary historian

PEASEBLOSSOM: Hail, mortal!

COBWEB: Hail!

MOTH: Hail!

MUSTARDSEED: Hail!   170

BOTTOM: I cry your worship's mercy, heartily. I beseech your worship's name.

COBWEB: Cobweb.

BOTTOM: I shall desire you of more acquaintance, good Master Cobweb. If I cut my finger, I shall make bold with you. Your name, honest gentleman?

PEASEBLOSSOM: Peaseblossom.

BOTTOM: I pray you, commend me to Mistress Squash, your Mother, and to Master Peascod, your father. Good Master Peaseblossom, I shall desire you of more   180 acquaintance too. Your name, I beseech you, sir?

MUSTARDSEED: Mustardseed.

BOTTOM: Good Master Mustardseed, I know your patience well. That same cowardly, giant-like ox-beef hath devoured many a gentleman of your house. I promise you, your kindred hath made my eyes water ere now. I desire your more acquaintance, good Master Mustardseed.

TITANIA: Come, wait upon him. Lead him to my bower.
The moon, methinks, looks with a watery eye,   190
And when she weeps, weeps every little flower,
Lamenting some enforced chastity.
Tie up my love's tongue, bring him silently.

Exeunt.

179. *Peascod* – a ripe peapod

189. *bower* – bed chamber
190 – 91. This refers to the dew on the flowers. It was believed that dew came down from the moon.

193. Titania instructs her fairies to silence the braying Bottom. Perhaps only her eyes have been affected by the magical flower.

Act Three
Scene 2

Another part of the wood.

Enter Oberon.

OBERON: I wonder if Titania be awaked;
Then, what it was that next came in her eye,
Which she must dote on in extremity.

Enter Puck.

Here comes my messenger. How now, mad spirit!
What night-rule now about this haunted grove?
PUCK: My mistress with a monster is in love.
Near to her close and consecrated bower,
While she was in her dull and sleeping hour,
A crew of patches, rude mechanicals,
That work for bread upon Athenian stalls,   10
Were met together to rehearse a play,
Intended for great Theseus' nuptial-day.
The shallowest thick-skin of that barren sort,
Who Pyramus presented, in their sport,
Forsook his scene, and entered in a brake,
When I did him at this advantage take.
An ass's nole I fixed on his head.
Anon his Thisbe must be answered,
And forth my mimic comes. When they him spy,
As wild geese that the creeping fowler eye,   20
Or russet-pated choughs, many in sort,
Rising, and cawing at the gun's report,
Sever themselves, and madly sweep the sky,

Puck gleefully informs Oberon that Titania has fallen in love with an ass. Puck and Oberon then overhear a conversation between Hermia and Demetrius and realize that the love-juice has been applied to the wrong person. When Hermia runs away, Demetrius falls asleep, Oberon applies the magical juice, Demetrius wakes up, and he falls in love with Helena. In the ensuing chaos, Demetrius and Lysander fight over Helena, who is convinced that they are playing a joke on her. Hermia thinks that Helena has betrayed her and seduced Lysander. When all four lovers are asleep, Puck applies the antidote to Lysander's eyes.

5. *What ... now* – "What has occurred during the night"
9. "A company of clowns and rough tradesmen"

13. Puck describes Bottom as the silliest (*shallowest*) of the dull-witted (*barren*) company. It was believed that a person's sensitivity could be measured by the thickness of the skin.

17. ass's nole – head of an ass
19. *mimic* – actor
20. *fowler* – bird hunter
21. "Or a large flock of drab-headed crows"
22. There were no guns in ancient Greece. See note on anachronisms on page 17.
23. *Sever* – scatter

53

25. To frighten his victims,
Puck stamps his feet.

27 – 28. "Their senses, made
weak by their strong fear,
caused them to be injured by
inanimate objects."

36. *latched* – moistened;
captured

43. *rebuke* – scold

44. *Lay breath* – use words

48 – 49. A proverbial
expression: someone who has
already waded into shallow
water (blood) may as well go
further and "plunge in the
deep."

51 – 55. Hermia is convinced
that Demetrius has murdered
Lysander. Rather than think
Lysander has left her, she
would more easily believe the
earth could be *bored* with a
hole so wide that the moon
(Diana) could creep through it
to the other side (the
Antipodes). This would
displease her brother, the sun
(Apollo), because he would
have to share the noonday sky
with her.

"The frame scenes [the first
and last scenes] of the play
contain specific time references which enable us to
date events, whereas the
magic wood scenes abound
in night images which
create confusion and
suggest one long uninter-
rupted dream. Time as
measured by the movement
of the sun disappears in the
enchanted wood."
– Anne Paolucci, American
playwright, poet, and
scholar

So, at his sight, away his fellows fly.
And at our stamp, here o'er and o'er, one falls.
He murder cries, and help from Athens calls.
Their sense thus weak, lost with their fears thus strong,
Made senseless things begin to do them wrong;
For briars and thorns at their apparel snatch.
Some sleeves, some hats, from yielders all things catch.   30
I led them on in this distracted fear,
And left sweet Pyramus translated there.
When in that moment, so it came to pass,
Titania waked, and straightway loved an ass.

OBERON: This falls out better than I could devise.
But hast thou yet latched the Athenian's eyes
With the love-juice, as I did bid thee do?

PUCK: I took him sleeping, that is finished too,
And the Athenian woman by his side,
That when he waked, of force she must be eyed.   40

Enter Demetrius and Hermia.

OBERON: Stand close. This is the same Athenian.

PUCK: This is the woman, but not this the man.

DEMETRIUS: O, why rebuke you him that loves you so?
Lay breath so bitter on your bitter foe.

HERMIA: Now I but chide, but I should use thee worse,
For thou, I fear, hast given me cause to curse.
If thou hast slain Lysander in his sleep,
Being o'er shoes in blood, plunge in the deep,
And kill me too.
The sun was not so true unto the day,   50
As he to me. Would he have stolen away
From sleeping Hermia? I'll believe as soon
This whole earth may be bored and that the moon
May through the centre creep, and so displease
Her brother's noontide with the Antipodes.
It cannot be but thou hast murdered him.
So should a murderer look, so dead, so grim.

DEMETRIUS: So should the murdered look, and so should I,
Pierced through the heart with your stern cruelty.
Yet you, the murderer, look as bright, as clear,   60
As yonder Venus in her glimmering sphere.

HERMIA: What's this to my Lysander? Where is he?
Ah good Demetrius, wilt thou give him me?

DEMETRIUS: I had rather give his carcass to my hounds.

HERMIA: Out dog, out cur! Thou drivest me past the bounds
 Of maiden's patience. Hast thou slain him then?
 Henceforth be never numbered among men.
 O, once tell true, tell true, even for my sake!
 Durst thou have looked upon him, being awake,
 And hast thou killed him sleeping? O brave touch! 70
 Could not a worm, an adder do so much?
 An adder did it. For with doubler tongue
 Than thine, thou serpent, never adder stung.

DEMETRIUS: You spend your passion on a misprised mood.
 I am not guilty of Lysander's blood.
 Nor is he dead, for aught that I can tell.

HERMIA: I pray thee, tell me then that he is well.

DEMETRIUS: And if I could, what should I get therefore?

HERMIA: A privilege never to see me more.
 And from thy hated presence part I so. 80
 See me no more, whether he be dead or no.

Exit [Hermia].

DEMETRIUS: There is no following her in this fierce vein.
 Here therefore for a while I will remain.
 So sorrow's heaviness doth heavier grow,
 For debt that bankrupt sleep doth sorrow owe.
 Which now in some slight measure it will pay,
 If for his tender here I make some stay.

Lies down [and sleeps.
Oberon and Puck come forward.]

OBERON: What hast thou done? Thou hast mistaken quite,
 And laid the love-juice on some true love's sight.
 Of thy misprision must perforce ensue 90
 Some true love turned, and not a false turned true.

PUCK: Then fate o'er-rules, that, one man holding troth,
 A million fail, confounding oath on oath.

OBERON: About the wood, go swifter than the wind,
 And Helena of Athens look thou find.
 All fancy-sick she is and pale of cheer,
 With sighs of love, that costs the fresh blood dear.
 By some illusion see thou bring her here.
 I'll charm his eyes against she do appear.

71. *a worm, an adder* – a snake, a poisonous snake

74. *misprised mood* – mistaken anger

82. *vein* – temper
84 – 87. Demetrius, exhausted by his heavy sorrow and lack of sleep, decides to rest.

90. *misprision* – error
91. *turned* – i.e., turned against the one that is loved
92 – 93. "Then fate will prove us wrong, for each man who keeps his vows, a million will break them over and over."

93. *confounding* – breaking
96. *fancy-sick* – lovesick

97. It was believed that with each sigh, a drop of blood was spent. In *Romeo and Juliet*, the audience is told that "Dry sorrow drinks our blood."

99. *against* – in preparation for when

101. *Tartar's bow* – This Asian bow was known for its power.
109. *remedy* – i.e., for his lovesickness
112. *youth* – i.e., Lysander
114. *fond* – foolish

"[Shakespeare,] like Puck, is vastly entertained by human follies. 'What fools these mortals be' might serve as a second title for the play, but there is nothing satirical or malicious in the playwright's laughter."
– Thomas Parrott, English scholar

"And those things do best please me, / That befall preposterously."

123. *come* – show themselves
125. *nativity* – birth
127. *badge* – In Shakespeare's day, servants wore badges as pledges of service to their masters.
128. *advance* – display
129. Lysander has vowed to love both Hermia and Helena. The truth of one vow, whichever it is, kills the other.
133. *tales* – fiction; lies

PUCK: I go, I go, look how I go.   100
        Swifter than arrow from the Tartar's bow.

Exit Puck.

OBERON: *[Squeezes the juice on Demetrius' eyes.]*
            Flower of this purple dye,
            Hit with Cupid's archery,
            Sink in apple of his eye.
            When his love he doth espy,
            Let her shine as gloriously
            As the Venus of the sky.
            When thou wak'st, if she be by,
            Beg of her for remedy.

Enter Puck.

PUCK: Captain of our fairy band,   110
            Helena is here at hand,
            And the youth, mistook by me,
            Pleading for a lover's fee.
            Shall we their fond pageant see?
            Lord, what fools these mortals be!
OBERON: Stand aside. The noise they make,
            Will cause Demetrius to awake.
PUCK: Then will two at once woo one;
            That must needs be sport alone.
            And those things do best please me,   120
            That befall preposterously.

Enter Lysander [following] Helena.

LYSANDER: Why should you think that I should woo in scorn?
        Scorn and derision never come in tears.
        Look when I vow, I weep; and vows so born,
        In their nativity all truth appears.
        How can these things in me, seem scorn to you,
        Bearing the badge of faith to prove them true?
HELENA: You do advance your cunning more and more.
        When truth kills truth, O devilish-holy fray!
        These vows are Hermia's. Will you give her o'er? 130
        Weigh oath with oath, and you will nothing weigh.
        Your vows to her, and me, put in two scales,
        Will even weigh, and both as light as tales.

LYSANDER: I had no judgment, when to her I swore.
HELENA: Nor none, in my mind, now you give her o'er.
LYSANDER: Demetrius loves her, and he loves not you.
DEMETRIUS: *[Awaking and seeing Helena.]*
    O Helen, goddess, nymph, perfect, divine!
    To what, my love, shall I compare thine eyne?
    Crystal is muddy. O, how ripe in show,
    Thy lips, those kissing cherries, tempting grow!   140
    That pure congealed white, high Taurus snow,
    Fanned with the eastern wind, turns to a crow,
    When thou hold'st up thy hand. O, let me kiss
    This princess of pure white, this seal of bliss!
HELENA: O spite! O hell! I see you all are bent
    To set against me, for your merriment.
    If you were civil, and knew courtesy,
    You would not do me thus much injury.
    Can you not hate me, as I know you do,
    But you must join in souls to mock me too?   150
    If you were men, as men you are in show,
    You would not use a gentle lady so.
    To vow, and swear, and superpraise my parts,
    When I am sure you hate me with your hearts.
    You both are rivals, and love Hermia;
    And now both rivals, to mock Helena.
    A trim exploit, a manly enterprise,
    To conjure tears up in a poor maid's eyes
    With your derision! None of noble sort
    Would so offend a virgin, and extort   160
    A poor soul's patience, all to make you sport.
LYSANDER: You are unkind, Demetrius; be not so.
    For you love Hermia. This you know I know.
    And here, with all good will, with all my heart,
    In Hermia's love I yield you up my part,
    And yours of Helena to me bequeath,
    Whom I do love, and will do till my death.
HELENA: Never did mockers waste more idle breath.
DEMETRIUS: Lysander, keep thy Hermia. I will none.
    If e'er I loved her, all that love is gone.   170
    My heart to her, but as guest-wise sojourned,
    And now to Helen is it home returned,
    There to remain.
LYSANDER: Helen, it is not so.

141. *Taurus* – a mountain range in present-day Turkey

144. *seal* – pledge
145 – 46. *bent ... set* – in a plot

150. *in souls* – heart and soul
156. *rivals* – can also mean *partners*

"Puck is a ... quick-change artist, a prestidigitator and producer of the comedy of errors. He confuses the couples of lovers and causes Titania to caress an ass's head. In fact, he makes them all ridiculous, Titania and Oberon no less than Hermia and Lysander, Helena and Demetrius. He exposes the folly of love. He is accident, fate, chance."
– Jan Kott (b. 1914), American scholar and Shakespearean critic

171. *guest-wise, sojourned* – Demetrius means that his heart left its true home (with Helena) and sojourned as a guest with Hermia.

175. *Disparage* – criticize
176. *aby* – pay for

178 – 83. Hermia's sense of hearing and not her sight enabled her to find Lysander in the dark night.

187. *bide* – stay
188. *engilds* – makes bright
189. *oes and eyes* – orbs or circles—in other words, stars
193. *confederacy* – plot
198. *bait* – torment. Bear-baiting was a popular Elizabethan sport. It involved tormenting a bear by tying it to a stake and setting dogs upon it.

bear-baiting

204. *artificial* – skilled in the arts and crafts
206. *sampler* – piece of embroidery
209. *incorporate* – as one body

DEMETRIUS: *[To Lysander.]*
 Disparage not the faith thou dost not know,
 Lest to thy peril, thou aby it dear.
 Look where thy love comes. Yonder is thy dear.

Enter Hermia.

HERMIA: Dark night, that from the eye his function takes,
 The ear more quick of apprehension makes.
 Wherein it doth impair the seeing sense,   180
 It pays the hearing double recompense.
 Thou art not by mine eye, Lysander, found.
 Mine ear, I thank it, brought me to thy sound.
 But why unkindly didst thou leave me so?
LYSANDER: Why should he stay, whom love doth press to go?
HERMIA: What love could press Lysander from my side?
LYSANDER: Lysander's love, that would not let him bide,
 Fair Helena, who more engilds the night
 Than all yon fiery oes and eyes of light.
 Why seek'st thou me? Could not this make thee know, 190
 The hate I bear thee, made me leave thee so?
HERMIA: You speak not as you think. It cannot be.
HELENA: Lo, she is one of this confederacy!
 Now I perceive, they have conjoined all three,
 To fashion this false sport, in spite of me.
 Injurious Hermia, most ungrateful maid!
 Have you conspired, have you with these contrived
 To bait me, with this foul derision?
 Is all the counsel that we two have shared,
 The sisters' vows, the hours that we have spent, 200
 When we have chid the hasty-footed time
 For parting us? O, is all forgot?
 All school-days' friendship, childhood innocence?
 We, Hermia, like two artificial gods,
 Have with our needles created both one flower,
 Both on one sampler, sitting on one cushion,
 Both warbling of one song, both in one key,
 As if our hands, our sides, voices and minds,
 Had been incorporate. So we grew together,
 Like to a double cherry, seeming parted,   210
 But yet an union in partition,
 Two lovely berries moulded on one stem;

So, with two seeming bodies, but one heart,
Two of the first, like coats in heraldry,
Due but to one, and crowned with one crest.
And will you rent our ancient love asunder,   216. *rent* – tear
To join with men in scorning your poor friend?
It is not friendly, 'tis not maidenly.
Our sex, as well as I, may chide you for it,   219. *Our sex* – every woman
Though I alone do feel the injury.   220

HERMIA: I am amazed at your passionate words.
I scorn you not: it seems that you scorn me.

HELENA: Have you not set Lysander, as in scorn,
To follow me, and praise my eyes and face?
And made your other love, Demetrius,
Who even but now did spurn me with his foot,
To call me goddess, nymph, divine, and rare,
Precious, celestial? Wherefore speaks he this,
To her he hates? And wherefore doth Lysander
Deny your love, so rich within his soul,   230
And tender me, forsooth, affection,   231. *tender* – offer
But by your setting on, by your consent?
What though I be not so in grace as you,   233. *in grace* – as popular
So hung upon with love, so fortunate,
But miserable most, to love unloved?
This you should pity rather than despise.

HERMIA: I understand not what you mean by this.

HELENA: Ay, do. Persever, counterfeit sad looks,   238. *sad* – serious
Make mouths upon me when I turn my back,   239. *mouths* – faces
Wink each at other, hold the sweet jest up.   240
This sport, well carried, shall be chronicled.   241. *be chronicled* – go down in history
If you have any pity, grace, or manners,
You would not make me such an argument.   243. *such an argument* – an object of such ridicule
But fare ye well. 'Tis partly my own fault,
Which death or absence soon shall remedy.

LYSANDER: Stay, gentle Helena. Hear my excuse.
My love, my life, my soul, fair Helena!   250. *entreat* – plead with you (to stop scorning Helena)

HELENA: O excellent!

HERMIA: *[To Lysander.]* Sweet, do not scorn her so.

DEMETRIUS: If she cannot entreat, I can compel.   250

LYSANDER: Thou canst compel no more than she entreat.
Thy threats have no more strength than her weak prayers.
Helen, I love thee, by my life, I do.
I swear by that which I will lose for thee,
To prove him false, that says I love thee not.

> "Only that which does not teach, which does not cry out, which does not condescend, which does not explain, is irresistible."
> – W. B. Yeats (1865–1939), Irish poet and dramatist

Act Three • Scene 2

DEMETRIUS: I say, I love thee more than he can do.

LYSANDER: If thou say so, withdraw, and prove it too.

DEMETRIUS: Quick, come.

HERMIA: Lysander, whereto tends all this?

LYSANDER: Away, you Ethiope! 260

DEMETRIUS: No, no. He'll
    Seem to break loose.

[To Lysander.]

            Take on as you would follow,
    But yet come not. You are a tame man, go!

LYSANDER: *[To Hermia.]*
    Hang off, thou cat, thou burr! Vile thing, let loose,
    Or I will shake thee from me like a serpent!

HERMIA: Why are you grown so rude? What change is this,
    Sweet love?

LYSANDER: Thy love! Out tawny Tartar, out!
    Out loathed medicine! O hated potion, hence!

HERMIA: Do you not jest? 270

HELENA: Yes sooth, and so do you.

LYSANDER: Demetrius, I will keep my word with thee.

DEMETRIUS: I would I had your bond, for I perceive
    A weak bond holds you. I'll not trust your word.

260. *Ethiope* – a reference to Hermia's darker complexion

261 – 62. Demetrius accuses Lysander of pretending to be ready to fight for Helena. Hermia, meanwhile, is clutching Lysander tightly and will not release him.

268. *tawny Tartar* – another reference to Hermia's darker complexion.

273. *bond* – signed pledge

274. *bond* – i.e., Hermia

60

LYSANDER: What, should I hurt her, strike her, kill her dead?
Although I hate her, I'll not harm her so.
HERMIA: What, can you do me greater harm, than hate?
Hate me? Wherefore? O me! What news, my love?
Am not I Hermia? Are not you Lysander?
I am as fair now as I was erewhile. 280
Since night you loved me; yet since night you left me.
Why then, you left me — O, the gods forbid! —
In earnest, shall I say?
LYSANDER: Ay, by my life,
And never did desire to see thee more.
Therefore be out of hope, of question, of doubt.
Be certain, nothing truer. 'Tis no jest
That I do hate thee and love Helena.
HERMIA: [To Helena.]
O me! You juggler, you canker-blossom!
You thief of love! What, have you come by night 290
And stolen my love's heart from him?
HELENA: Fine, in faith!
Have you no modesty, no maiden shame,
No touch of bashfulness? What, will you tear
Impatient answers from my gentle tongue?
Fie, fie, you counterfeit, you puppet, you!

RELATED READING
Hermia – literary essay by
Sarojini Shintri (page 119)

280. *erewhile* – a short while
ago

283. *In earnest* – intentionally

289. *juggler* – trickster
289. *canker-blossom* – grub
that infects blossoms

canker-blossom

308. *curst* – shrewish; difficult to get along with

310. *right* – proper

317. *counsels* – secrets

324. *folly* – foolish self

326. *fond* – friendly; foolish

337. *flout* – insult

HERMIA: "Puppet"? Why so? Ay, that way goes the game.
Now I perceive that she hath made compare
Between our statures. She hath urged her height,
And with her personage, her tall personage,   300
Her height, forsooth, she hath prevailed with him.
And are you grown so high in his esteem,
Because I am so dwarfish and so low?
How low am I, thou painted maypole? Speak.
How low am I? I am not yet so low
But that my nails can reach unto thine eyes.

HELENA: I pray you, though you mock me, gentlemen,
Let her not hurt me. I was never curst.
I have no gift at all in shrewishness.
I am a right maid for my cowardice.   310
Let her not strike me. You perhaps may think,
Because she is something lower than myself,
That I can match her.

HERMIA: Lower? Hark again.

HELENA: Good Hermia, do not be so bitter with me.
I evermore did love you, Hermia,
Did ever keep your counsels, never wronged you,
Save that, in love unto Demetrius,
I told him of your stealth unto this wood.
He followed you; for love I followed him.   320
But he hath chid me hence, and threatened me
To strike me, spurn me, nay, to kill me too.
And now, so you will let me quiet go,
To Athens will I bear my folly back,
And follow you no further. Let me go.
You see how simple and how fond I am.

HERMIA: Why, get you gone. Who is it that hinders you?

HELENA: A foolish heart, that I leave here behind.

HERMIA: What, with Lysander?

HELENA: With Demetrius.   330

LYSANDER: Be not afraid. She shall not harm thee, Helena.

DEMETRIUS: No, sir, she shall not, though you take her part.

HELENA: O, when she's angry, she is keen and shrewd!
She was a vixen when she went to school,
And though she be but little, she is fierce.

HERMIA: "Little" again? Nothing but "low" and "little"?
Why will you suffer her to flout me thus?
Let me come to her.

LYSANDER: Get you gone, you dwarf,
    You minimus, of hindering knot-grass made.   340
    You bead, you acorn.
DEMETRIUS: You are too officious
    In her behalf that scorns your services.
    Let her alone. Speak not of Helena.
    Take not her part. For if thou dost intend
    Never so little show of love to her,
    Thou shalt aby it.
LYSANDER: Now she holds me not.
    Now follow, if thou darest, to try whose right,
    Of thine or mine, is most in Helena.   350
DEMETRIUS: Follow? Nay, I'll go with thee, cheek by jowl.

        Exeunt Lysander and Demetrius.

HERMIA: You, mistress, all this coil is long of you.
    Nay, go not back.
HELENA: I will not trust you, I,
    Nor longer stay in your curst company.
    Your hands than mine are quicker for a fray,
    My legs are longer though, to run away.

          Exit Helena.

HERMIA: I am amazed, and know not what to say.

          Exit Hermia.

OBERON: This is thy negligence. Still thou mistak'st,
    Or else committ'st thy knaveries wilfully.   360
PUCK: Believe me, king of shadows, I mistook.
    Did not you tell me I should know the man,
    By the Athenian garments he had on?
    And so far blameless proves my enterprise,
    That I have 'nointed an Athenian's eyes,
    And so far am I glad it so did sort,
    As this their jangling I esteem a sport.
OBERON: Thou see'st these lovers seek a place to fight.
    Hie therefore, Robin, overcast the night.
    The starry welkin cover thou anon,   370
    With drooping fog as black as Acheron,

340. *minimus* – smallest of tiny creatures
342. *officious* – overly preoccupied

351. *cheek by jowl* – side by side

352. *coil ... you* – all this turmoil is your fault

356. *fray* – fight

364. *blameless ... enterprise* – I am innocent in my efforts to serve you
367. *jangling* – fighting; squabbling
369. *Hie* – hurry
370. *welkin* – sky
371. *Acheron* – river running through the underworld (Hades)

378. *death-counterfeiting sleep* – sleep that could pass for death

381. *virtuous* – powerful

383. *wonted* – his accustomed

386. *wend* – make their way

387. *league* – friendship; amity

393. *night's swift dragons* – Just as the sun travels across the sky in a chariot pulled by fiery steeds, so does the moon travel, pulled by *swift dragons*.

394. *Aurora's harbinger* – the planet Venus, also known as the morning star. Aurora was the goddess of the dawn.

396 – 97. *Damned spirits* – spirits of suicides, whose bodies were often buried at crossroads *(crossways)* or remained in the rivers where they had drowned *(floods)*.

401. *aye* – ever

409. *effect* – complete

"To end the state of crisis … in Oberon's determination, at least, Titania's wayward spirit must be tempered. As for the lovers, Hermia must come to comprehend loss, Helena gain. Lysander must understand the vows of fidelity, and Demetrius the rewards of stability. In short, the lovers must learn that their understanding of love is fundamentally superficial … In the woods, each will discover that the greatest obstacles to love are … their own insufficiencies."
– Florence Falk, English scholar

And lead these testy rivals so astray
As one come not within another's way.
Like to Lysander, sometime frame thy tongue,
Then stir Demetrius up with bitter wrong.
And sometime rail thou like Demetrius,
And from each other, look thou lead them thus,
Till o'er their brows, death-counterfeiting sleep,
With leaden legs, and batty wings doth creep.
Then crush this herb into Lysander's eye,   380
Whose liquor hath this virtuous property,
To take from thence all error, with his might,
And make his eyeballs roll with wonted sight.
When they next wake, all this derision
Shall seem a dream, and fruitless vision,
And back to Athens shall the lovers wend,
With league, whose date till death shall never end.
Whiles I in this affair do thee employ,
I'll to my queen and beg her Indian boy,
And then I will her charmed eye release   390
From monster's view, and all things shall be peace.

PUCK: My fairy lord, this must be done with haste,
For night's swift dragons cut the clouds full fast,
And yonder shines Aurora's harbinger,
At whose approach ghosts, wandering here and there,
Troop home to churchyards. Damned spirits all,
That in crossways and floods have burial,
Already to their wormy beds are gone;
For fear lest day should look their shames upon,
They wilfully themselves exile from light,   400
And must for aye consort with black-browed night.

OBERON: But we are spirits of another sort.
I with the morning's love have oft made sport,
And like a forester, the groves may tread,
Even till the eastern gate, all fiery-red,
Opening on Neptune, with fair blessed beams,
Turns into yellow gold, his salt green streams.
But notwithstanding, haste; make no delay.
We may effect this business, yet ere day.

[Exit Oberon.]

PUCK: Up and down, up and down,   410
               I will lead them up and down.

I am feared in field and town.
Goblin, lead them up and down.
Here comes one.

Enter Lysander.

LYSANDER: Where art thou, proud Demetrius? Speak thou now.
PUCK: Here villain, drawn and ready. Where art thou?
LYSANDER: I will be with thee straight.
PUCK: Follow me, then,
    To plainer ground.

[Exit Lysander, following the voice.]
Enter Demetrius.

DEMETRIUS: Lysander! Speak again.   420
    Thou runaway, thou coward, art thou fled?
    Speak! In some bush? Where dost thou hide thy head?
PUCK: Thou coward, art thou bragging to the stars,
    Telling the bushes that thou look'st for wars,
    And wilt not come? Come recreant, come thou child.   425. *recreant* – coward
    I'll whip thee with a rod. He is defiled
    That draws a sword on thee.
DEMETRIUS: Yea, art thou there?
PUCK: Follow my voice. We'll try no manhood here.   429. *try* – test

Exeunt.
Enter Lysander.

LYSANDER: He goes before me, and still dares me on.   430
    When I come where he calls, then he is gone.
    The villain is much lighter-heeled than I.
    I followed fast, but faster he did fly.
    That fallen am I in dark uneven way,
    And here will rest me.

[Lies down.]

            Come, thou gentle day.
    For if but once thou show me thy grey light,
    I'll find Demetrius and revenge this spite.

[Sleeps.]

RELATED READING

To Puck – poem by
Beatrice Llewellyn
Thomas (page 124)

Act Three • Scene 2

Enter Puck and Demetrius.

PUCK: Ho, ho, ho! Coward, why com'st thou not?

DEMETRIUS: Abide me, if thou darest, for well I wot,
Thou runn'st before me, shifting every place,   440
And dar'st not stand, nor look me in the face.
Where art thou now?

PUCK: Come hither. I am here.

DEMETRIUS: Nay then thou mock'st me. Thou shalt buy this
dear,
If ever I thy face by daylight see.
Now, go thy way. Faintness constraineth me
To measure out my length on this cold bed.
By day's approach look to be visited.

[Lies down and sleeps.]
Enter Helena.

HELENA: O weary night, O long and tedious night,
Abate thy hours! Shine comforts from the east,   450
That I may back to Athens, by daylight,
From these that my poor company detest.
And sleep, that sometimes shuts up sorrow's eye,
Steal me awhile from mine own company.

[Helena lies down and] sleeps.

PUCK: Yet but three? Come one more,
Two of both kinds make up four.
Here she comes, curst and sad.
Cupid is a knavish lad,
Thus to make poor females mad.

Enter Hermia.

HERMIA: Never so weary, never so in woe,   460
Bedabbled with the dew and torn with briars,
I can no further crawl, no further go.
My legs can keep no pace with my desires.
Here will I rest me till the break of day.
Heavens shield Lysander, if they mean a fray!

[Hermia lies down and sleeps.]

439. *Abide* – wait for
439. *wot* – know

450. *Abate* – cut short

454. *Steal* – liberate; take

"Hermia collapses from exhaustion with her last conscious thought a prayer for Lysander's safety: 'Heaven shield Lysander …' When she awakes, her constancy and faith are rewarded. The events of the confused night in the woods are a test of character as well as love, and one which Hermia passes more impressively than do her companions."
– Raymond B. Waddington (b. 1935), American scholar, University of California

PUCK: On the ground
           Sleep sound.
           I'll apply
           To your eye,
       Gentle lover, remedy.   470

[Puck squeezes the juice on Lysander's eyes.]

           When thou wak'st,
           Thou tak'st
           True delight
           In the sight
       Of thy former lady's eye.
     And the country proverb known,
    That every man should take his own,
    In your waking shall be shown:
           Jack shall have Jill,
           Nought shall go ill.   480
   The man shall have his mare again,
           And all shall be well.

[Exit Puck. The lovers remain, asleep.]

❧ ❧ ❧

The four lovers remain sleeping on stage until they are wakened midway through the next scene.

Act Three Considerations

ACT THREE Scene 1

▶ The actors agree that two prologues should be written to explain and excuse the "fearful" elements in their play. Are the actors justified in believing that the prologues are necessary? Explain.

      Write one of these prologues, following Bottom's advice that each line should contain eight syllables.

▶ Much of the comic effect of this scene depends on irony. In groups, list all the examples of irony that you can find in this scene. Do you think Bottom knows that he has been transformed? Explain.

▶ Like Helena in the previous scene, Bottom discovers that he is the object of someone's adulation. How does his reaction to the discovery compare with Helena's? What does his reaction reveal about his personality?

▶ It is important for the reader or audience to appreciate that Bottom's transformation is not only comical but also grotesque. If you were directing this play, what advice would you give to the actor playing Bottom about how to play the part after the transformation?

ACT THREE Scene 2

▶ In this scene, Puck describes (lines 6 to 34) what the audience already knows. In groups, discuss why Shakespeare might have included this lengthy speech. What effect might he have been trying to create?

▶ It has been said that Oberon is a friend to lovers. Summarize the evidence in this scene that supports this view.

▶ During the chaotic scene between the four lovers, Oberon and Puck remain on stage, visible to the audience but silent. If you were directing this play, what instructions would you give to the actors playing Oberon and Puck to make their silent presence interesting to the audience?

▶ What are we told of the longstanding relationship between Hermia and Helena? What upsets Helena the most about Hermia in this scene? Why does Hermia become so upset? To what extent do young people today act in similar ways to Shakespeare's sixteenth-century characters?

▶ Demetrius' plight at the beginning of the scene is interesting. Write a paragraph discussing which is worse: to like someone who doesn't feel the same way about you, or to be chased by someone you are not at all interested in.

▶ Puck maintains that he is most pleased by things that "befall preposterously." Study the woodcut on page 54 and write short sentences that identify what is preposterous about each image in the graphic. Using magazine illustrations, original artwork, or both, create a series of preposterous things that might please Puck. Select common modern phrases that deal with the preposterous to label your graphics.

▶ Imagine that you are a famous daytime talk show host interviewing the four lovers at the point when Demetrius and Lysander are in love with Helena and when Helena and Hermia are puzzled by the recent turns of affection in the two males. Create a compelling title for the day's topic. You may use the model: "Friends who …" Then, in a series of questions and answers, interview the two couples in such a way as to review the information provided in this scene and to encourage them to predict what might happen next in their relationships.

Act Three Considerations

Act Four
Scene 1

The wood.

Lysander, Demetrius, Helena, and Hermia lying asleep.
Enter Titania, Queen of the Fairies, and Bottom; Peaseblossom,
Cobweb, Moth, Mustardseed, and other Fairies attending;
Oberon, the King of the Fairies, behind [unseen].

TITANIA: Come, sit thee down upon this flowery bed,
While I thy amiable cheeks do coy,
And stick musk-roses in thy sleek smooth head,
And kiss thy fair large ears, my gentle joy.
BOTTOM: Where's Peaseblossom?
PEASEBLOSSOM: Ready.
BOTTOM: Scratch my head, Peaseblossom. Where's Moun-
sieur Cobweb?
COBWEB: Ready.
BOTTOM: Mounsieur Cobweb, good mounsieur, get you   10
your weapons in your hand, and kill me a red-hipped
humble-bee on the top of a thistle, and, good mounsieur,
bring me the honey-bag. Do not fret yourself too much
in the action, mounsieur, and good mounsieur have a
care the honey-bag break not. I would be loath to have
you overflown with a honey-bag, signior. Where's
Mounsieur Mustardseed?
MUSTARDSEED: Ready.
BOTTOM: Give me your neaf, Mounsieur Mustardseed. Pray
you, leave your courtesy, good mounsieur.   20
MUSTARDSEED: What's your will?
BOTTOM: Nothing, good mounsieur, but to help Cavalery
Cobweb to scratch. I must to the barber's, mounsieur, for
methinks I am marvellous hairy about the face, and I am
such a tender ass, if my hair do but tickle me, I must
scratch.

While Oberon remains hidden, Titania expresses her love for Bottom before they fall asleep. Oberon then removes the spell from Titania's eyes and when she awakes, the sight of Bottom repels her. Puck removes the ass's head from Bottom. Theseus, Hippolyta, and Egeus come upon the sleeping pairs of lovers. Theseus overrules Egeus and invites the lovers back to Athens to be married in the temple with himself and Hippolyta. Bottom awakes, believing that he has had an incredible dream.

2. *coy* – stroke

19. *neaf* – hand
20. *leave your courtesy* – stop
bowing to me

71

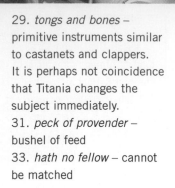

29. *tongs and bones* – primitive instruments similar to castanets and clappers. It is perhaps not coincidence that Titania changes the subject immediately.

31. *peck of provender* – bushel of feed

33. *hath no fellow* – cannot be matched

38. *exposition of* – Bottom likely means "disposition to."

40. *all ways* – in every direction

41 – 43. Titania entwines her arms around Bottom.

49. *upbraid* – confront with criticisms
fall out – argued

51. *coronet* – small crown

55. *bewail* – mourn; weep

TITANIA: What, wilt thou hear some music, my sweet love?

BOTTOM: I have a reasonable good ear in music. Let's have the tongs and the bones.

TITANIA: Or say, sweet love, what thou desirest to eat. 30

BOTTOM: Truly a peck of provender. I could munch your good dry oats. Methinks I have a great desire to a bottle of hay. Good hay, sweet hay hath no fellow.

TITANIA: I have a venturous fairy that shall seek
The squirrel's hoard, and fetch thee new nuts.

BOTTOM: I had rather have a handful or two of dried peas. But, I pray you, let none of your people stir me. I have an exposition of sleep come upon me.

TITANIA: Sleep thou, and I will wind thee in my arms.
Fairies, be gone, and be all ways away. 40

[Exeunt fairies.]

So doth the woodbine, the sweet honeysuckle,
Gently entwist; the female ivy so
Enrings the barky fingers of the elm.
O how I love thee! How I dote on thee!

[They sleep.]
Enter Puck.

OBERON: *[Advancing.]*
Welcome, good Robin. See'st thou this sweet sight?
Her dotage now I do begin to pity,
For, meeting her of late behind the wood,
Seeking sweet favours from this hateful fool,
I did upbraid her, and fall out with her.
For she his hairy temples then had rounded 50
With a coronet of fresh and fragrant flowers.
And that same dew, which sometime on the buds
Was wont to swell, like round and orient pearls,
Stood now within the pretty flowerets' eyes
Like tears that did their own disgrace bewail.
When I had, at my pleasure, taunted her.
And she in mild terms begged my patience,
I then did ask of her, her changeling child;
Which straight she gave me, and her fairy sent
To bear him to my bower in fairy land. 60
And now I have the boy, I will undo
This hateful imperfection of her eyes.
And, gentle Puck, take this transformed scalp,

From off the head of this Athenian swain,
That he, awaking when the other do,
May all to Athens back again repair,
And think no more of this night's accidents,
But as the fierce vexation of a dream.
But first I will release the fairy queen.

[Squeezes the juice of the flower on Titania's eyelids.]

Be as thou wast wont to be;   70
See as thou wast wont to see.
Dian's bud o'er Cupid's flower
Hath such force and blessed power.
Now, my Titania, wake you, my sweet queen.
TITANIA: My Oberon! What visions have I seen!
Methought I was enamoured of an ass.
OBERON: There lies your love.
TITANIA: How came these things to pass?
O, how mine eyes do loathe his visage now!
OBERON: Silence awhile. Robin, take off this head.   80
Titania, music call; and strike more dead
Than common sleep, of all these five the sense.
TITANIA: Music, ho music, such as charmeth sleep!

Music, still.

PUCK: Now, when thou wak'st, with thine own fool's eyes
peep.
OBERON: Sound, music!

[Oberon and Titania strike up a dance.]

Come, my queen, take hands with me,
And rock the ground whereon these sleepers be.
Now thou and I are new in amity,
And will tomorrow midnight, solemnly
Dance in Duke Theseus' house triumphantly,
And bless it to all fair prosperity.   90
There shall the pairs of faithful lovers be
Wedded, with Theseus, all in jollity.
PUCK: Fairy king, attend, and mark:
I do hear the morning lark.
OBERON: Then, my queen, in silence sad,
Trip we after the night's shade.
We, the globe can compass soon,
Swifter than the wandering moon.

64. *swain* – lover

And dreaming through the
twilight
That doth not rise nor
set,
Haply I may remember,
And haply may forget.
– Christina Rossetti
(1830–94), English poet

79. *visage* – face

81 – 82. Oberon instructs
Puck to induce a deeper
sleep in the four lovers.

87. *amity* – friendship

Beautiful dreamer wake
unto me,
Starlight and dewdrop are
waiting for thee.
– Traditional Lullaby

97. *compass* – circle

73

TITANIA: Come, my lord, and in our flight
Tell me how it came this night,   100
That I sleeping here was found
With these mortals on the ground.

[Exeunt Oberon and Titania.]
The four lovers and Bottom still lie asleep.
[To the winding of horns, within],
enter Theseus, Hippolyta, Egeus, and Train.

104. *observation* – May Day
ceremonial rites
105. *vaward* – earliest part of
the morning
107. *Uncouple* – release

THESEUS: Go, one of you, find out the forester.
For now our observation is performed,
And since we have the vaward of the day,
My love shall hear the music of my hounds.
Uncouple in the western valley. Let them go.
Dispatch I say, and find the forester.

[Exit an Attendant.]

110 – 11. They will listen to
the blending of sounds that
the barking and the echoes
of barking will create.
112. *Cadmus* – legendary
founder of Thebes
113. *Crete* – island in the
eastern Mediterranean. See
the map on page 12.
113. *bayed* – cornered
114. *Sparta* – city-state of
ancient Greece. See the map
on page 12.

We will, fair queen, up to the mountain's top,
And mark the musical confusion   110
Of hounds and echo in conjunction.
HIPPOLYTA: I was with Hercules and Cadmus once,
When in a wood of Crete they bayed the bear
With hounds of Sparta. Never did I hear
Such gallant chiding. For, besides the groves,

The skies, the fountains, every region near
Seemed all one mutual cry. I never heard
So musical a discord, such sweet thunder.

THESEUS: My hounds are bred out of the Spartan kind,
So flewed, so sanded, and their heads are hung 120
With ears that sweep away the morning dew,
Crook-knee'd, and dew-lapped like Thessalian bulls;
Slow in pursuit, but matched in mouth like bells,
Each under each. A cry more tuneable
Was never holla'd to, nor cheered with horn,
In Crete, in Sparta, nor in Thessaly:
Judge when you hear. But, soft! What nymphs are these?

EGEUS: My lord, this is my daughter here asleep,
And this, Lysander; this Demetrius is,
This Helena, old Nedar's Helena. 130
I wonder of their being here together.

THESEUS: No doubt they rose up early to observe
The rite of May, and hearing our intent,
Came here, in grace of our solemnity.
But speak, Egeus. Is not this the day
That Hermia should give answer of her choice?

EGEUS: It is, my lord.

THESEUS: Go, bid the huntsmen wake them with their horns.

Shout within; winding of horns.
The lovers [awake, startled].

120. *So flewed, so sanded* –
having the same large,
hanging cheeks and sandy-
brown hue

122. *Crook-knee'd, and dew-
lapped* – having bent legs
and large folds of skin under
their chins

122. *Thessalian* – Thessaly is
in northern Greece. See the
map on page 12.

134. *in ... solemnity* – to
grace our ceremony

139 – 40. It was believed that birds picked their mates on St. Valentine's Day.

144. *concord* – peace

"I slept and dreamed that life was Beauty;
I woke and found that life was duty."
– Ellen S. Hooper
(1816–41), English poet

164. *fancy* – love
165. *wot* – know

168. *idle gaud* – worthless toy

RELATED READING

Forgotten Dreams –
poem by Edward Silvera
(page 125)

174. *a sickness* – a person who is sick
180. Theseus does what in Act One, Scene 1 he claimed he could not do. He chooses not to uphold the law and overrules Egeus' will.
183. *for* – since

Good morrow, friends. Saint Valentine is past.
Begin these wood-birds but to couple now? 140
LYSANDER: Pardon, my lord.
THESEUS: I pray you all, stand up.
I know you two are rival enemies.
How comes this gentle concord in the world,
That hatred is so far from jealousy,
To sleep by hate, and fear no enmity?
LYSANDER: My lord, I shall reply amazedly,
Half sleep, half waking. But as yet, I swear,
I cannot truly say how I came here,
But, as I think — for truly would I speak, 150
And now do I bethink me, so it is —
I came with Hermia hither. Our intent
Was to be gone from Athens, where we might,
Without the peril of the Athenian law —
EGEUS: Enough, enough my lord. You have enough!
I beg the law, the law, upon his head!
They would have stolen away, they would, Demetrius,
Thereby to have defeated you and me.
You of your wife, and me of my consent,
Of my consent, that she should be your wife. 160
DEMETRIUS: My lord, fair Helen told me of their stealth,
Of this their purpose hither, to this wood,
And I in fury hither followed them,
Fair Helena, in fancy following me.
But my good lord, I wot not by what power, —
But by some power it is, — my love to Hermia,
Melted as the snow, seems to me now
As the remembrance of an idle gaud
Which in my childhood I did dote upon;
And all the faith, the virtue of my heart, 170
The object and the pleasure of mine eye,
Is only Helena. To her, my lord,
Was I betrothed ere I saw Hermia.
But, like a sickness, did I loathe this food.
But, as in health, come to my natural taste,
Now I do wish it, love it, long for it,
And will for evermore be true to it.
THESEUS: Fair lovers, you are fortunately met.
Of this discourse, we more will hear anon.
Egeus, I will overbear your will. 180
For in the temple, by and by, with us,
These couples shall eternally be knit.
And, for the morning now is something worn,

Our purposed hunting shall be set aside.
Away, with us to Athens. Three and three,
We'll hold a feast, in great solemnity.
Come, Hippolyta.

Exeunt Theseus, Hippolyta, Egeus, and Train.

DEMETRIUS: These things seem small and undistinguishable,
Like far-off mountains turned into clouds.
HERMIA: Methinks I see these things with parted eye,   190
When everything seems double.
HELENA: So methinks.
And I have found Demetrius like a jewel,
Mine own, and not mine own.
DEMETRIUS: Are you sure
That we are awake? It seems to me
That yet we sleep, we dream. Do not you think
The Duke was here, and bid us follow him?
HERMIA: Yea, and my father.
HELENA: And Hippolyta.   200
LYSANDER: And he did bid us follow to the temple.
DEMETRIUS: Why then, we are awake. Let's follow him
And by the way let us recount our dreams.

Exeunt.

BOTTOM: [*Awaking*]
When my cue comes, call me, and I will answer. My next
is, "Most fair Pyramus." Heigh-ho! Peter Quince? Flute,
the bellows-mender? Snout, the tinker! Starveling? God's
my life! Stolen hence, and left me asleep! I have had a
most rare vision. I have had a dream, past the wit of
man, to say, what dream it was. Man is but an ass, if he
go about to expound this dream. Methought I was —   210
there is no man can tell what. Methought I was, — and
methought I had, — but man is but a patched fool, if he
will offer to say what methought I had. The eye of man
hath not heard, the ear of man hath not seen, man's hand
is not able to taste, his tongue to conceive, nor his heart
to report, what my dream was. I will get Peter Quince to
write a ballad of this dream. It shall be called "Bottom's
Dream," because it hath no Bottom; and I will sing it in
the latter end of a play, before the Duke. Peradventure,
to make it the more gracious, I shall sing it at her death.

Exit.

77

190. *parted* – unfocused

210. *expound* – explain
212. *patched fool* – motley clown
213 – 19. In the Geneva Bible (1557), the version Shakespeare would have read, is the following: "The eye hath not seen, and the ear hath not heard, neither have entered into the heart of man, the things which God hath prepared for them that love him. But God hath opened them unto us by his spirit. For the spirit searcheth all things, ye the bottom of God's secrets" (Corinthians 2: 9 – 10).
219. *Peradventure* – perhaps

RELATED READING

A Most Rare Vision – literary essay by Norrie Epstein (page 126)

"Bottom, it might be argued, is not confusing his senses nor misquoting Scripture. Having mentioned the eye first, it does not matter to him that the remainder of the vehicles of sense and their perceptions are mismatched, because all senses are subject to sight, and he has had the ultimate vision of the play."
– Helen Peters, Canadian scholar

Act Four
Scene 2

Athens. Quince's house.

Enter Quince, Flute, Snout, and Starveling.

QUINCE: Have you sent to Bottom's house? Is he come home yet?

STARVELING: He cannot be heard of. Out of doubt he is transported.

FLUTE: If he come not, then the play is marred. It goes not forward, doth it?

QUINCE: It is not possible. You have not a man in all Athens able to discharge Pyramus but he.

FLUTE: No, he hath simply the best wit of any handicraft man in Athens.   10

QUINCE: Yea, and the best person too, and he is a very paramour, for a sweet voice.

FLUTE: You must say, "paragon." A paramour is, God bless us, a thing of naught.

Enter Snug the Joiner.

SNUG: Masters, the Duke is coming from the temple, and there is two or three lords and ladies more married. If our sport had gone forward, we had all been made men.

FLUTE: O sweet bully Bottom! Thus hath he lost sixpence a day during his life. He could not have 'scaped sixpence a day. And the Duke had not given him sixpence a day for   20 playing Pyramus, I'll be hanged. He would have deserved it. Sixpence a day, in Pyramus, or nothing.

Enter Bottom.

4. *transported* – Bottom is not the only one to use wrong words. Starveling likely means to say "transformed." Yet Bottom was indeed transported—from the human realm to fairy land.

12 – 14. Flute corrects Quince for saying *paramour* (a naughty or wicked person) instead of *paragon* (a model of perfection).

17. *made men* – Their fortunes would have been made because in recognition for their service, they would have been granted a lifetime pension.
20. *And* – if

BOTTOM: Where are these lads? Where are these hearts?

QUINCE: Bottom! O most courageous day! O most happy hour!

BOTTOM: Masters, I am to discourse wonders. But ask me not what. For if I tell you, I am no true Athenian. I will tell you everything, right as it fell out.

QUINCE: Let us hear, sweet Bottom.

BOTTOM: Not a word of me. All that I will tell you is, that   30
the Duke hath dined. Get your apparel together, good strings to your beards, new ribbons to your pumps. Meet presently at the palace. Every man look o'er his part, for the short and the long is, our play is preferred. In any case, let Thisbe have clean linen, and let not him that plays the lion pare his nails, for they shall hang out for the lion's claws. And most dear actors, eat no onions, nor garlic, for we are to utter sweet breath. And I do not doubt but to hear them say, it is a sweet comedy. No
more words. Away! Go away!   40

Exeunt.

ᘓ ᘓ ᘓ

Act Four Considerations

ACT FOUR Scene 1

▶ On the surface, the relationship between Bottom and Titania is similar to that between Beauty and the Beast. Review the famous fairy tale. What other similarities are there between the two stories? What are the major differences?

▶ When Titania awakes, free of the magic spell, she asks Oberon how it came to pass that she was in love with an ass. Oberon does not answer, but it is implied that he will. Write a short scene in which Oberon reveals to his wife what happened. How do you think Titania responds to the revelation?

▶ Demetrius suggests (line 203) that they recount their dreams as they make their way toward Athens. Write or improvise a short scene between the two couples during which they share their recollections of their respective dreams. Remember that, despite the commonality of their "dream," each had different experiences during the night.

ACT FOUR Scene 2

▶ The mechanicals seem upset about Bottom's disappearance. How sincere do you think they are in their praise of Bottom at the beginning of this scene? What other reasons could they have for speaking so highly of Bottom?

▶ Why does Bottom not tell his friends about his dream? Do you think he ever gets Quince to write a ballad of his dream, as he suggests in Act Four, Scene 1? If you were Bottom and wanted Quince to write the ballad, on what elements of your fairyland experience would you want Quince to focus?

Act Five
Scene 1

Athens. The palace of Theseus.

Enter Theseus and Hippolyta;
Philostrate, Lords, and Attendants.

HIPPOLYTA: 'Tis strange, my Theseus, that these lovers
    speak of.
THESEUS: More strange than true. I never may believe
    These antique fables, nor these fairy toys.
    Lovers and madmen have such seething brains,
    Such shaping fantasies, that apprehend
    More than cool reason ever comprehends.
    The lunatic, the lover, and the poet
    Are of imagination all compact.
    One sees more devils than vast hell can hold.
    That is the madman. The lover, all as frantic,   10
    Sees Helen's beauty in a brow of Egypt.
    The poet's eye, in fine frenzy rolling,
    Doth glance from heaven to earth, from earth to heaven.
    And as imagination bodies forth
    The forms of things unknown, the poet's pen
    Turns them to shapes and gives to airy nothing
    A local habitation and a name.
    Such tricks hath strong imagination,
    That if it would but apprehend some joy,
    It comprehends some bringer of that joy.   20
    Or in the night, imagining some fear,
    How easy is a bush supposed a bear?
HIPPOLYTA: But, all the story of the night told over,
    And all their minds transfigured so together,
    More witnesseth than fancy's images,
    And grows to something of great constancy.
    But howsoever, strange and admirable.

The three couples have just been married and have dined. Theseus and Hippolyta discuss the story the lovers told of their night in the forest. Despite Philostrate's protests, Theseus chooses the play *Pyramus and Thisbe* as their evening's entertainment. The artisans put on a comically inept show, which pleases the newlyweds. After the humans have gone to bed, Puck, Oberon, Titania, and the fairies bless the house and all its inhabitants.

3. *antique* – ancient; quaint. *Antic*, which sounds similar, means absurd.
3. *toys* – idle fantasies
4. *seething* – overactive
5. "Such creative imaginations that perceive"
8. *compact* – of the same form
11. *Helen* – Helen of Troy was considered the most beautiful woman in the ancient Greek world.
11. *of Egypt* – of a gypsy

12. *fine frenzy* – Poets were considered to be inspired from above, infused with a divine madness.

14. *bodies forth* – translates into familiar forms
24. *transfigured so together* – affected in the same way

"The exchange between the bridegroom and his acutely perceptive but eternally overshadowed bride amounts to the first critical discussion of the play.... The debate seems one-sided in the duke's favor, but how could we fail ... to realize that the real last word belongs to Hippolyta, both literally and figuratively?...
– René Girard (b. 1923), French scholar

33. *masques* – elaborate entertainments

41. *abridgement* – entertainment that will make long hours seem shorter or that has been shortened
44. *brief* – list with brief summaries
46. *Centaurs* – mythical creatures, half horse and half human

centaur

49. *kinsman* – Theseus was Hercules' cousin.
50. *Bacchanals* – followers of Bacchus, the Greek god of wine, some of whom in their revelling tore Orpheus *(the Thracian singer)* to pieces.

THESEUS: Here come the lovers, full of joy and mirth.

*Enter the lovers: Lysander and Hermia,
Demetrius and Helena.*

Joy, gentle friends, joy and fresh days of love
Accompany your hearts!   30
LYSANDER: More than to us
Wait in your royal walks, your board, your bed!
THESEUS: Come now. What masques, what dances shall we
        have,
To wear away this long age of three hours
Between our after-supper and bed-time?
Where is our usual manager of mirth?
What revels are in hand? Is there no play,
To ease the anguish of a torturing hour?
Call Philostrate.
PHILOSTRATE: Here, mighty Theseus.   40
THESEUS: Say, what abridgement have you for this evening?
What masque, what music? How shall we beguile
The lazy time, if not with some delight?
PHILOSTRATE: There is a brief how many sports are ripe.
Make choice of which your highness will see first.

[Giving a paper.]

THESEUS: *[Reads.]*
"The battle with the Centaurs, to be sung
By an Athenian eunuch, to the harp."
We'll none of that. That have I told my love,
In glory of my kinsman Hercules.

[Reads.]

"The riot of the tipsy Bacchanals,   50
Tearing the Thracian singer in their rage."
That is an old device, and it was played
When I from Thebes came last a conqueror.

[Reads.]

"The thrice three Muses mourning for the death
Of Learning, late deceased in beggary."
That is some satire, keen and critical,
Not sorting with a nuptial ceremony.

[Reads.]

"A tedious brief scene of young Pyramus
And his love Thisbe, very tragical mirth."
Merry and tragical? Tedious and brief?   60
That is hot ice, and wondrous strange snow.
How shall we find the concord of this discord?
PHILOSTRATE: A play there is, my lord, some ten words long,
 Which is as brief as I have known a play.
 But by ten words, my lord, it is too long,
 Which makes it tedious. For in all the play,
 There is not one word apt, one player fitted,
 And tragical, my noble lord, it is.
 For Pyramus, therein, doth kill himself.
 Which when I saw rehearsed, I must confess,   70
 Made mine eyes water; but more merry tears
 The passion of loud laughter never shed.
THESEUS: What are they that do play it?
PHILOSTRATE: Hard-handed men, that work in Athens here,
 Which never laboured in their minds till now,
 And now have toiled their unbreathed memories,
 With this same play, against your nuptial.
THESEUS: And we will hear it.
PHILOSTRATE: No, my noble lord,
 It is not for you. I have heard it over,   80
 And it is nothing, nothing in the world,
 Unless you can find sport in their intents,
 Extremely stretched and conned with cruel pain,
 To do you service.
THESEUS: I will hear that play,
 For never anything can be amiss,
 When simpleness and duty tender it.
 Go bring them in, and take your places, ladies.

[Exit Philostrate.]

HIPPOLYTA: I love not to see wretchedness o'er charged,
 And duty in his service perishing.   90
THESEUS: Why, gentle sweet, you shall see no such thing.
HIPPOLYTA: He says they can do nothing in this kind.
THESEUS: The kinder we, to give them thanks for nothing.
 Our sport shall be to take what they mistake.
 And what poor duty cannot do, noble respect
 Takes it in might, not merit.
 Where I have come, great clerks have purposed

54. *Muses* – The Greeks believed that the sciences and arts were the domain of the nine Muses, goddesses who inspired epic, love, sacred, and lyric poetry; tragedy; comedy; choral dance and song; history; and astronomy.

57. *sorting* – appropriate
61. *hot ice* – Theseus' phrase *hot ice* is an oxymoron, a rhetorical device that combines two words that are opposite in meaning. The term oxymoron is made up of two Greek words that mean "sharp" and "dull."
70. It is not clear when Philostrate could have watched a rehearsal. See note on p. 79, Act Four, Scene 2.
76. *unbreathed* – not trained

82. *intents* – attempts
83. *conned* – memorized
86. *amiss* – wrong
87. *tender* – offer
89 – 90. Hippolyta does not want to see the tradespeople so overburdened that their efforts to please fail.

92. That is, they cannot act.
95 – 96. *respect ... merit* – Theseus suggests that they will appreciate what the actors might be able to do, rather than what they actually do.
97. *clerks* – scholars

Act Five • Scene 1

100. *periods* – awkward pauses

101. "Choke with fear while delivering rehearsed speeches"

104 – 109. Theseus contends that people need not give a polished performance in showing their duty and respect. Their *tongue-tied,* faltering speeches please him more than the elegant words of insincere subjects.

109. *capacity* – way of thinking

112 – 21. Quince has the punctuation in this speech wrong, and the result is nonsense. The comma at the end of line 121 is intentional, as it implies that the Prologue has lost his train of thought.

116. *but in despite* – only to displease you

117. *as minding* – intending

119. *repent you* – regret

122. *points* – punctuation

124. *stop* – period; pause

127. *government* – control

129. *impaired* – broken

RELATED READINGS

Pyramus and Thisbe – myth by Edith Hamilton (page 129)

To greet me with premeditated welcomes;
Where I have seen them shiver and look pale,
Make periods in the midst of sentences,   100
Throttle their practised accent in their fears,
And in conclusion dumbly have broke off,
Not paying me a welcome. Trust me, sweet,
Out of this silence, yet, I picked a welcome,
And in the modesty of fearful duty,
I read as much as from the rattling tongue
Of saucy and audacious eloquence.
Love, therefore, and tongue-tied simplicity,
In least, speak most, to my capacity.

[Enter Philostrate.]

PHILOSTRATE: So please your grace, the Prologue is addressed.   110
THESEUS: Let him approach.

Flourish of trumpets.
Enter the Prologue, Quince.

PROLOGUE: *If we offend, it is with our good will.*
That you should think, we come not to offend,
But with good will. To show our simple skill,
That is the true beginning of our end.
Consider then, we come but in despite.
We do not come, as minding to content you,
Our true intent is. All for your delight,
We are not here. That you should here repent you,
The actors are at hand; and by their show,   120
You shall know all, that you are like to know,

THESEUS: This fellow doth not stand upon points.
LYSANDER: He hath rid his prologue, like a rough colt. He knows not the stop. A good moral, my lord. It is not enough to speak, but to speak true.
HIPPOLYTA: Indeed he hath played on his prologue, like a child on a recorder, a sound, but not in government.
THESEUS: His speech was like a tangled chain. Nothing impaired, but all disordered. Who is next?

Enter with a trumpeter before them:
[Bottom as] Pyramus, and [Flute as] Thisbe,
and [Snout as] Wall, and [Starveling as] Moonshine,
and [Snug as] Lion.

PROLOGUE: *Gentles, perchance you wonder at this show.*   130
          But wonder on, till truth make all things plain.
          This man is Pyramus, if you would know;
          This beauteous lady Thisbe is certain.
          This man, with lime and rough-cast, doth present
          Wall, that vile Wall which did these lovers sunder;
          And through Wall's chink, poor souls, they are content
          To whisper. At the which, let no man wonder.
          This man, with lantern, dog, and bush of thorn,
          Presenteth Moonshine. For if you will know,
          By moonshine did these lovers think no scorn   140
          To meet at Ninus' tomb, there, there to woo.
          This grisly beast, which Lion hight by name,
          The trusty Thisbe, coming first by night,
          Did scare away, or rather did affright;
          And as she fled, her mantle she did fall,
          Which Lion vile with bloody mouth did stain.
          Anon comes Pyramus, sweet youth, and tall,
          And finds his trusty Thisbe's mantle slain.
          Whereat, with blade, with bloody blameful blade,
          He bravely broached his boiling bloody breast.   150
          And Thisbe, tarrying in mulberry shade,
          His dagger drew, and died. For all the rest,
          Let Lion, Moonshine, Wall, and lovers twain
          At large discourse, while here they do remain.

          [Exeunt Prologue, Pyramus, Thisbe, Lion,
          and Moonshine.]

THESEUS: I wonder if the lion be to speak.
DEMETRIUS: No wonder, my lord. One lion may, when
          many asses do.

WALL: *In this same interlude it doth befall*
       That I, one Snout by name, present a wall;
       And such a wall, as I would have you think,   160
       That had in it a crannied hole or chink,
       Through which the lovers, Pyramus and Thisbe,

135. *sunder* – separate; keep apart
136. *chink* – hole; crack

140. *think no scorn* – not think it shameful
142. *hight* – is called

145. *mantle* – scarf

149 – 50. In this excessive use of alliteration, Shakespeare parodies other dramatists' abuse of the device.

150. *broached* – pierced
151. *tarrying* – waiting

153. *twain* – both
154. *At large discourse* – talk about at length

The nobles use prose rather than verse as they joke about the performance. See page 10 of the Introduction about Shakespeare's verse.

158. *interlude* – entertainment

Act Five • Scene 1

Did whisper often, very secretly.
This loam, this rough-cast, and this stone doth show,
That I am that same wall. The truth is so:
And this the cranny is, right and sinister,
Through which the fearful lovers are to whisper.

THESEUS: Would you desire lime and hair to speak better?
DEMETRIUS: It is the wittiest partition that ever I heard
    discourse, my lord.   170

Enter Pyramus.

THESEUS: Pyramus draws near the wall. Silence!

PYRAMUS: *O grim-looked night! O night with hue so black!*
    O night, which ever art when day is not!
    O night, O night! Alack, alack, alack!
    I fear my Thisbe's promise is forgot!
    And thou O wall, O sweet, O lovely wall,
    That stand'st between her father's ground and mine!
    Thou wall, O wall, O sweet and lovely wall,
    Show me thy chink, to blink through with mine eyne!

[Wall holds up his fingers
through which Pyramus peers.]

180. *Jove* – the chief god of
the Romans
184 – 85. "The wall, having
sensibilities, should curse
back."

Thanks, courteous wall. Jove shield thee well for this! 180
But what see I? No Thisbe do I see.
O wicked wall, through whom I see no bliss!
Cursed be thy stones for thus deceiving me!

THESEUS: The wall, methinks, being sensible, should curse
    again.
PYRAMUS: No, in truth, sir, he should not. "Deceiving me"
    is Thisbe's cue. She is to enter now, and I am to spy her
    through the wall. You shall see, it will fall pat as I told
    you. Yonder she comes.

186. Bottom commits the
greatest sin of all for an actor
—he steps out of character and
directly addresses the audience
when it is not called for in the
script.

Enter Thisbe.

THISBE: *O wall, full often hast thou heard my moans,* 190
    For parting my fair Pyramus and me!
    My cherry lips have often kissed thy stones,
    Thy stones, with lime and hair knit up in thee.

PYRAMUS: *I see a voice. Now will I to the chink,*
    To spy and I can hear my Thisbe's face.
    Thisbe!
THISBE: *My love thou art, my love I think.*
PYRAMUS: *Think what thou wilt, I am thy lover's grace.*
    And, like Limander, am I trusty still.
THISBE: *And I like Helen, till the Fates me kill.*   200
PYRAMUS: *Not Shafalus to Procrus was so true.*
THISBE: *As Shafalus to Procrus, I to you.*
PYRAMUS: *O kiss me through the hole of this vile wall!*
THISBE: *I kiss the wall's hole, not your lips at all.*
PYRAMUS: *Wilt thou at Ninny's tomb meet me straightway?*
THISBE: *'Tide life, 'tide death, I come without delay.*

      Exeunt Pyramus and Thisbe [in different directions].

WALL: *Thus have I, Wall, my part discharged so;*
    And, being done, thus Wall away doth go.

              Exit Wall.

THESEUS: Now is the mural down between the two
    neighbours.   210
DEMETRIUS: No remedy, my lord, when walls are so wilful
    to hear without warning.
HIPPOLYTA: This is the silliest stuff that ever I heard.
THESEUS: The best in this kind are but shadows, and the
    worst are no worse, if imagination amend them.
HIPPOLYTA: It must be your imagination then, and not
    theirs.
THESEUS: If we imagine no worse of them than they of
    themselves, they may pass for excellent men. Here
    come two noble beasts in, a man and a lion.

          Enter Lion and Moonshine.

LION: *You, ladies, you, whose gentle hearts do fear*   220
    The smallest monstrous mouse that creeps on floor,
    May now, perchance, both quake and tremble here,
    When lion rough in wildest rage doth roar.
    Then know that I, one Snug the joiner, am
    A lion-fell, nor else no lion's dam.
    For, if I should as lion come in strife
    Into this place, 'twere pity on my life.

194 – 95. Bottom sees a voice and he goes to hear a face. The technical term for this mixing of the senses is *synesthesia.*

195. *and* – if
199 – 201. *Limander ... Helen* – Bottom and Flute probably mean to say Leander and Hero, lovers whose story ends tragically.
201. *Shafalus to Procrus* – a mistaken reference to Cephalus and Procrus, another pair of faithful but ill-fated lovers.

RELATED READING

A World Upside Down – literary essay by Marchette Chute (page 132)

206. *'Tide* come
209. *mural* – wall
214. *shadows* – Actors were commonly referred to as *shadows*, in that they are but pale reflections of reality.
215. *amend them* – make up for what they lack

"Hippolyta is consistently Theseus's informant in the play and indeed Egeus might have done well to appeal to her judgment rather than his at the beginning."
– Ruth Nevo, American scholar

RELATED READING

The Bottomless Dream – literary essay by Northrop Frye (page 134)

225. *lion-fell* – cruel lion

Act Five • Scene 1

231. A goose is noted for its stupidity rather than its *discretion* or courage.
232. *carry* – exceed

237. *horned* – crescent

240. *circumference* – full circle or moon

247. *in snuff* – needing to be put out; in an angry mood

"In the play within the play, the fun puts both players and audience together inside the jest of professional actors pretending to be mechanicals trying to be amateur actors before an unreal audience."
– Muriel C. Bradbrook (b. 1909), British Elizabethan scholar

THESEUS: A very gentle beast, and of a good conscience.
DEMETRIUS: The very best at a beast, my lord, that e'er I saw.
LYSANDER: This lion is a very fox for his valour.   230
THESEUS: True, and a goose for his discretion.
DEMETRIUS: Not so my lord. For his valour cannot carry his discretion; and the fox carries the goose.
THESEUS: His discretion, I am sure, cannot carry his valour; for the goose carries not the fox. It is well. Leave it to his discretion, and let us listen to the moon.

MOONSHINE: *This lantern doth the horned moon present;* —

DEMETRIUS: He should have worn the horns on his head.
THESEUS: He is no crescent, and his horns are invisible, within the circumference.   240

MOONSHINE: *This lantern doth the horned moon present;*
Myself, the man in the moon, do seem to be.

THESEUS: This is the greatest error of all the rest. The man should be put into the lantern. How is it else the man in the moon?
DEMETRIUS: He dares not come there for the candle. For, you see, it is already in snuff.
HIPPOLYTA: I am aweary of this moon. Would he would change!
THESEUS: It appears, by his small light of discretion, that he   250
is in the wane; but yet, in courtesy, in all reason, we must stay the time.
LYSANDER: Proceed, Moon.
MOONSHINE: All that I have to say, is, to tell you, that the lantern is the moon, I the man in the moon, this thorn-bush my thorn-bush, and this dog my dog.
DEMETRIUS: Why, all these should be in the lantern, for all these are in the moon. But, silence! Here comes Thisbe.

Enter Thisbe.

THISBE: *This is old Ninny's tomb. Where is my love?*
LION: *Oh* ——   260

[The Lion roars; Thisbe runs off,
after dropping her mantle.]

DEMETRIUS: Well roared Lion.

THESEUS: Well run Thisbe.

HIPPOLYTA: Well shone Moon. Truly, the moon shines with a good grace.

[The Lion shakes Thisbe's mantle, and exit.]

THESEUS: Well moused, Lion.

DEMETRIUS: And then came Pyramus.

LYSANDER: And so the lion vanished.

Enter Pyramus.

PYRAMUS: *Sweet Moon, I thank thee, for thy sunny beams.*
I thank thee, Moon, for shining now so bright.
For, by thy gracious, golden, glittering gleams,   270
I trust to take of truest Thisbe sight.
     But stay, O spite!
     But mark, poor knight,
What dreadful dole is here!
     Eyes, do you see?
     How can it be?
O dainty duck! O dear!
     Thy mantle good,
     What, stained with blood!
Approach, ye Furies fell!   280
     O Fates, come, come,
     Cut thread and thrum;
Quail, crush, conclude, and quell!

THESEUS: This passion, and the death of a dear friend, would go near to make a man look sad.

HIPPOLYTA: Beshrew my heart, but I pity the man.

PYRAMUS: *O wherefore, Nature, didst thou lions frame,*
Since lion vile hath here deflowered my dear?
Which is — no, no — which was the fairest dame
That lived, that loved, that liked, that looked with cheer.   290
     Come tears, confound!
     Out sword, and wound
The pap of Pyramus!
     Ay, that left pap,
     Where heart doth hop.

[Stabs himself.]

274. *dole* – cause for sorrow

"In the 'Pyramus' segment ... overinflated writing, bad acting, obtrusive theatrical props, naive remarks addressed to the spectators all serve to turn the tragical history into a farce ... a story that, were it played 'straight,' would rival *Romeo and Juliet* in effect."
– Barbara A. Mowat, American scholar

280. *Furies fell* – cruel instruments of justice
281. *Fates* – the three goddesses who control human destiny
282. "Cut everything or end life"

"Shakespeare seems to have constructed in *Dream* the 'worst case' for theatre, voicing all the attacks on drama being made in his time and deliberately showing plays, actors and audiences at their worst. And since 'the best in this kind are but shadows,' *Pyramus and Thisbe* seems to indict all plays, including *A Midsummer Night's Dream*, as mere rant of awkward actors and unrealistic dreaming of frenzied poets."
– Alvin B. Kernan (b. 1923), American scholar

291. *confound* – confuse; destroy
293. *pap* – breast

Act Five • Scene 1

303. *die* – the singular form of *dice*
303. *ace* – play on words

312. *use a long one* – deliver a long, passionate speech
314 – 15. "A minute speck will tip the scales as to whether Pyramus is better than Thisbe."
315. *warrant* – help
318. "And thus she moans, as follows"

Thus die I, thus, thus, thus.
  Now am I dead,
  Now am I fled.
My soul is in the sky.
  Tongue, lose thy light,   300
  Moon take thy flight!

[Exit Moonshine.]

Now die, die, die, die, die.

[Dies.]

DEMETRIUS: No die, but an ace for him. For he is but one.
LYSANDER: Less than an ace, man. For he is dead; he is nothing.
THESEUS: With the help of a surgeon, he might yet recover, and prove an ass.
HIPPOLYTA: How chance Moonshine is gone before Thisbe comes back and finds her lover?
THESEUS: She will find him, by starlight.   310

Enter Thisbe.

Here she comes, and her passion ends the play.
HIPPOLYTA: Methinks, she should not use a long one for such a Pyramus. I hope she will be brief.
DEMETRIUS: A mote will turn the balance, which Pyramus, which Thisbe, is the better. He for a man, God warrant us; she for a woman, God bless us.
LYSANDER: She hath spied him already, with those sweet eyes.
DEMETRIUS: And thus she means, videlicet —

THISBE: *Asleep, my love?*
          What, dead, my dove?   320
      O Pyramus, arise,
          Speak, speak. Quite dumb?
          Dead, dead? A tomb
      Must cover thy sweet eyes.
          These lily lips,
          This cherry nose,
      These yellow cowslip cheeks,
          Are gone, are gone!

Lovers, make moan!
His eyes were green as leeks. 330
O Sisters Three,
Come, come, to me,
With hands as pale as milk,
Lay them in gore,
Since you have shore
With shears his thread of silk.
Tongue, not a word!
Come, trusty sword,
Come blade, my breast imbrue!

[Stabs herself.]

And farewell friends!
Thus Thisbe ends! 340
Adieu, adieu, adieu!

[Dies.]

THESEUS: Moonshine and Lion are left to bury the dead.
DEMETRIUS: Ay, and Wall too.
BOTTOM: *[Standing up.]*
No, I assure you; the wall is down that parted their fathers. Will it please you to see the epilogue, or to hear a Bergomask dance, between two of our company?
THESEUS: No epilogue, I pray you. For your play needs no excuse. Never excuse. For when the players are all dead, there needs none to be blamed. Marry, if he that writ it had played Pyramus and hanged himself in Thisbe's 350 garter, it would have been a fine tragedy. And so it is, truly; and very notably discharged. But come, your Bergomask. Let your epilogue alone.

[Enter Quince, Snug, Snout, and Starveling. A dance.]

The iron tongue of midnight hath told twelve.
Lovers to bed, 'tis almost fairy time.
I fear we shall out-sleep the coming morn,
As much as we this night have overwatched.
This palpable-gross play hath well beguiled
The heavy gait of night. Sweet friends, to bed.
A fortnight hold we this solemnity, 360
In nightly revels, and new jollity.

Exeunt.

330. *leeks* – The leek, a common vegetable, resembles a large green onion.
331. *Sisters Three* – the three Fates
335. *shore* – shorn; cut
339. *imbrue* – make bloody

347. A bergomask was a farcical dance imitating the movements of the peasants of the Bergamo area in Italy.

"The bergomask most likely displays not the ineptitude but rather the skill of the 'rude mechanicals.'"
– Skiles Howard, American Tudor dance scholar

348. The tradition in the epilogue was to offer apologies and ask the audience to excuse the shortcomings of the performance.

RELATED READING

Song — for Epilogue – song by David Garrick (page 136)

355. *told* – tolled; struck

"When Theseus leads the bridal couples to bed ... with the mocking reminder that 'tis almost fairy time, he intends the remark as a last jibe [at the lovers]. The joke, however, is on Theseus. It is indeed almost fairy time."
– Anne Barton, English scholar, University of Oxford

359. *palpable-gross* – clearly crude
360. *gait* – pace; passage
361. *solemnity* – festivities

Act Five • Scene 1

Enter Puck.

PUCK:　Now the hungry lion roars,
　　　　And the wolf behowls the moon;
　　　　Whilst the heavy ploughman snores,
　　　　All with weary task fordone.
　　　　Now the wasted brands do glow,
　　　　Whilst the screech-owl, screeching loud,
　　　　Puts the wretch that lies in woe,
　　　　In remembrance of a shroud.　　　　　　　370
　　　　Now it is the time of night,
　　　　That the graves, all gaping wide,
　　　　Every one lets forth his sprite,
　　　　In the church-way paths to glide.
　　　　And we fairies, that do run,
　　　　By the triple Hecate's team,
　　　　From the presence of the sun,
　　　　Following darkness like a dream,
　　　　Now are frolic. Not a mouse
　　　　Shall disturb this hallowed house.　　　　380
　　　　I am sent, with broom before,
　　　　To sweep the dust, behind the door.

*Enter Oberon and Titania,
with all their train.*

365. *heavy* – with sleep
366. *fordone* – exhausted
367. *wasted brands* – burnt-out logs
370. "Into brooding about death." A *shroud* is used to wrap a corpse.
373. *sprite* – spirit; ghost
376. *triple Hecate* – Hecate, the goddess of magic and witchcraft, had three distinct identities: as Cynthia or Luna in her sky aspect; as Diana on earth; and as Hecate or Proserpine in her underworld realm.
381. Robin Goodfellow was often depicted carrying a broom with which to sweep houses during the night while all within were asleep.

Act Five • Scene 1

OBERON: Through the house give gathering light,
By the dead and drowsy fire,
Every elf and fairy sprite,
Hop as light as bird from briar,
And this ditty after me,
Sing and dance it trippingly.

TITANIA: First rehearse your song by rote,
To each word a warbling note.   390
Hand in hand, with fairy grace,
Will we sing and bless this place.

[Song and dance.]

OBERON: Now, until the break of day,
Through this house, each fairy stray.
To the best bride-bed will we,
Which by us shall blessed be;
And the issue, there create,
Ever shall be fortunate.
So shall all the couples three
Ever true in loving be;   400
And the blots of Nature's hand
Shall not in their issue stand.
Never mole, hare-lip, nor scar,
Nor mark prodigious, such as are
Despised in nativity,

383. *gathering* – glimmering. The train of fairies most likely carried candles on their heads as they danced. Titania says in line 391 that they dance "hand in hand."

387. *ditty* – song
389. *rote* – memory

RELATED READING

A Midsummer Noon in the Australian Forest – poem by Charles Harpur (page 138)

397. *issue* – children

401. *blots* – blemishes; defects

404. *mark prodigious* – unlucky birthmark

Shall upon their children be.
With this field-dew consecrate,
Every fairy take his gait,
And each several chamber bless,
Through this palace, with sweet peace;   410
And the owner of it blest,
Ever shall in safety rest.
Trip away. Make no stay.
Meet me all by break of day.

Exeunt [all but Puck].

PUCK: If we shadows have offended,
Think but this, and all is mended,
That you have but slumbered here,
While these visions did appear.
And this weak and idle theme,
No more yielding but a dream,   420
Gentles, do not reprehend.
If you pardon, we will mend.
And, as I am an honest Puck,
If we have unearned luck,
Now to 'scape the serpent's tongue,
We will make amends, ere long;
Else the Puck a liar call.
So, good night unto you all.
Give me your hands, if we be friends,
And Robin shall restore amends.   430

FINIS.

413. *stay* – delay

415 – 30. Puck speaks the epilogue to the play.

419. *theme* – play; argument
420. *yielding* – of value; informative
421. *reprehend* – criticize

425. *serpent's tongue* – hissing; sounds of disapproval

429. *Give ... hands* – applaud

Act Five Considerations

ACT FIVE Scene 1

▶ This scene opens with Theseus expressing an opinion about the imaginations of lunatics, lovers, and poets. Summarize briefly his point of view. To what extent do you agree with him? Explain fully.

▶ According to the Greeks, the arts and sciences were the domain of the Muses. (See the note for line 54 of this scene.) Many Greek myths and modern stories contain references to the Muses and their interactions with humans. Using the Internet, CD-ROM, or the library, research one of the nine Muses and prepare a short report on her influence on human culture and learning.

▶ In his speech at lines 95 to 109, Theseus says that he prefers simple and honest shows of respect over polished performances. What other opinions does he express in this speech? If you were a member of Quince's company of actors and knew of Theseus' views, how would you feel? Explain fully.

▶ Quince is the playwright of the company, probably the most literate of the rude mechanicals and most likely the author of their "tedious and brief scene," including the opening prologue (lines 112 to 121). Yet in reciting the prologue, he mangles it. Read Quince's prologue carefully, paying special attention to the punctuation. Put the speech, as he speaks it, into your own words. Then choose another speech of four to ten lines from the play and change the punctuation so as to create a comical effect. You need not change the words. Read your revised versions to the class.

▶ During their performance, Pyramus and Thisbe mention two pairs of ill-fated lovers: Hero and Leander, and Cephalus and Procrus. Research the mythological stories of one of these pairs. Retell the story in a modern setting.

▶ Throughout the performance of Pyramus and Thisbe, Hermia and Helena do not speak. How do you account for their silence? Why might Shakespeare have them remain silent?

▶ The night of the wedding festivities has been a time of joy and celebration. Puck's speech (lines 363 to 382) brings in images that contrast sharply with the mood of preceding events. List the images and briefly describe the atmosphere they create. Why might Shakespeare have had Puck introduce such a mood at this point in the play? Explain fully.

▶ Oberon's speech at the end of the play (lines 393 to 412) creates the impression that everyone involved will live happily ever after and that even the children of the newly married couples will be blessed and fortunate. Was this the case? Research what myth tells of the subsequent fate of Theseus and Hippolyta.

Ten Challenging Questions about *A Midsummer Night's Dream*

Shakespeare's works have survived for over 400 years. His plays continue to be read, studied, performed, and enjoyed by people all over the world. Shakespeare's legacy is a host of unforgettable characters in great stories, speaking classic lines that contain some of the most powerful poetry ever written.

Perhaps another important reason why Shakespeare continues to fascinate readers and audiences is that his plays can be interpreted in so many different ways. It is ironic that Shakespeare's greatest strength is perhaps his most frustrating quality.

The play *A Midsummer Night's Dream* poses a number of very interesting and challenging questions. Choose one or more of the following for closer focus and study. The result of your efforts may take the form of a research essay, an independent study project, or a position paper. To address these questions, you will need to probe the text carefully and consult secondary sources.

1. What ideas does Theseus' speech about the lunatic, the lover, and the poet (5.1.4–22) develop regarding the imagination of the poet? To what extent is Theseus a lover of the arts and an admirer of the products of the imagination? Consider the whole play in responding to this question.

2. The play presents a number of different views about love. For each of the characters who are involved in any kind of love relationship, summarize what you think he or she believes about love. Then choose two of your summaries that you feel strongly contrast with each other. Write two position papers that present arguments in support of each view of love. Incorporate quotations and details from the play to help develop the arguments.

3. Much of what is believed today about fairies comes from Shakespeare. Research the history and evolution of fairies before Shakespeare's time. Then research Shakespeare's treatment of fairies in this and his other plays. How does Shakespeare's treatment of fairies compare with the view of fairies held before his time?

4. What difficulties does choosing a cast to perform this play present? Explain fully. How would you deal with these difficulties?

5. What do the scenes involving the rude mechanicals reveal about how plays were put on during Shakespeare's day? He seems to be poking fun at his fellow actors and playwrights. Research theatre life in Shakespeare's time. According to your research, was this comical treatment warranted?

6. Some scholars maintain that Bottom is pompous, overbearing, and foolish, before and after his magical transformation. He can also be seen in a more positive light, however. Compile a list of his least and most admirable qualities. Then write a character sketch in which you consider the full scope of Bottom's personality.

7. This play is unusual in that there is no one central character who can be considered the hero or protagonist. Who do you think comes closest to being the protagonist? Explain fully.

8. Outline the significant similarities and differences in the story of Pyramus and Thisbe and that of Lysander and Hermia? Do you think *A Midsummer Night's Dream* would have been appropriate entertainment for a wedding feast?

9. Shakespeare used a number of sources to write his play. See page 7 of the Introduction for these sources. Locate one or more of the sources to research more carefully. To what extent was Shakespeare faithful to his sources? What significant changes did he make to them? Do you agree with the changes that he made? Explain.

10. The play contains many speeches that feature lists of details. These details create a sense of realism in an unrealistic story.
    Find as many speeches as you can that contain a list of things. Then create titles for each list — for example, Seven Things Fairies Do While Their Queen Is Asleep. Once you have a title, use phrases from the speech to compile a list. Add, delete, or change words to make items consistent with each other. Find or create illustrations to accompany your lists.

Winter Moon

In her first speech in the play, Hippolyta describes the moon as a "silver bow, / New-bent in heaven." American poet Langston Hughes (1902–67) echoes this sentiment in the following poem.

How thin and sharp is the moon tonight!

How thin and sharp and ghostly white

Is the slim curved crook of the moon tonight

by Langston Hughes

The word "moon" occurs almost thirty times in this play. With each occurrence of the word, Shakespeare creates an evocative image. Using Hughes's work as a model and Shakespeare's images for inspiration, write your own poem about the moon. Find or create an illustration to go with the poem.

by Henry Miller

American novelist Henry Miller (1891–1980) calls this play a surrealistic, or dreamlike, paean. To the Greeks, a paean was a song of triumph or joy whose primary effect was to heal, to make people feel better. This is an excerpt from a letter Miller wrote in May 1936.

On Seeing
A Midsummer Night's Dream

Curious, how the other night in looking at the film, *Midsummer Night's Dream*, I felt much closer to Shakespeare than ever before. I came and turned to your *Encyclopaedia Britannica* to discover a little about the genesis of the play and when exactly it was written. I learned practically nothing. What prompted me was a conviction that this must have been written when Shakespeare was at his prime in a moment of full affluence, of health, success and well-being. Here was a surrealistic paean to the night life, a rollicking, reckless tribute to the powers of the Unconscious. Here the poet stepped forth again—*to prove nothing*. A free fantasia in which even Bottom fails to point a moral. And such a jumble! The idiotic Duke of Athens, the English Greeks, the false columns, the whole decor borrowed from a handbook of history for children. Of them all I like Oberon the best. Oberon the night rider!

He comes forward through the gloom of the brake clad like one of the black knights in the Arthurian legends. Behind him the billowing batwings, the smoke and doom, the ghostly web-like touch of dream....

This is the first time in my life that I enjoyed a Shakespearean spectacle, and I know now why. It is because I was just able to ignore the words. For when Shakespeare talks it is empty prattle to me, but when he nods, when he dreams, then do I follow him—and with a vengeance. Here we leave the realm of truth and moral to enter the realm of music—the only realm ... which is truly satisfying, complete in itself and requiring no interpretation. This is a seeing into the heart of things with eyes shut. You close your eyes ... and then, because of a vibration inaccessible to the understanding ... it results that all the secrets of the heart which logic had stopped now pour out and inundate the world. ∎

What does Miller seem to like most about this play? What enabled him to enjoy the performance? Despite his praise, he also has a number of criticisms of the play. What are they?

Do you agree or disagree with Miller's views of the play? Explain.

THESEUS and the UNHAPPY MAN

by Robert Watson

Why does Theseus side with Egeus in compelling Hermia to marry Demetrius? In this selection, which takes place immediately prior to the action in Shakespeare's play, British novelist Robert Watson provides an answer. He also explains the curious connection between Theseus and Bottom.

One warm afternoon a great lord, fresh from victory, reined in his horse, thus bringing to a noisy halt his tough returning army, and gazing thoughtfully into the gentle valley just beyond the forest—gazing at the only part of the bowled landscape not flickering with the sun's heat—he said:

"I see there is one who cannot be happy."

Those near enough to catch this remark repeated it carefully, and as it was passed along the lines the wonder increased, for no one in the entire train could make out a living soul in that green shaded valley below the road. A few stony clusters of sheep were grazing on the far slope under a walled olive grove, and they were as stiff as gravestones, but all that could be seen of unhappy humanity was the pathetic handiwork of the remoter working-folk, a few rough shacks thrown up with wood and straw and held together with dung. Such dwellings were beneath the notice of the many brave knights in the great lord's company, and yet it seemed that he did indeed gaze towards these rudimentary blots.

"My lord," the young knight Demetrius felt invited to ask, "where can you discern unhappiness? We see no sign."

The governor sighed, not without a certain restrained satisfaction. "Look again, Demetrius, and tell me what your eye says."

Polite and petted Demetrius scanned the unpromising area intently, anxious to impress his master, as were the others who copied him. Everyone within earshot wished to participate. The object lessons in good government so freely given by their renowned lord were never taken lightly, however loopy they seemed to be. The knights knew that their own children, and their children's children, would learn the saws by heart and bless the memory of the ancestor sensible enough to pass them on. In this way all his fawning retinue praised their lord for shedding his assured immortality upon them, sometimes twice or thrice a day.

Related Readings

Now Demetrius was ready with his report. "I see the welcoming familiar light that Phoebus has cast for our safe return, and, lapped in its gaze, enriched by my fond gazing, I see the simple meadows I played in as a child, I see the well-stocked wood where the glad hart has multiplied unchecked in our absence to promise better sport and even greater feasts than hitherto."

"Bravo, Demetrius!"

"Well spoke, Demetrius!"

"But seriously, boy, don't you see those cottages too?"

"I was ashamed to acknowledge them in this context, my lord."

"You're too fastidious. Acknowledge them now, if you please, as directly as you can."

"Then, sir," Demetrius said stumblingly, "it's true, the rural seat of humble swains falls within our purview, and we accept that together with the cattle and sheep and forest their purpose is to serve the general good, which is to say the good of those of us whose business it is to rule … er … for which wide bounty I give thanks to … to …" He blushed deeply. "I cannot recall a deity to thank for the existence of such poor creatures as dwell down there—forgive me, lord."

The governor smiled comfortably at his lieutenant's discomfiture. "It strikes me that ever since we could smell land again your senses have gone doolally—maybe that explains the nancy diction. You were smitten with old Nedar's daughter once, if I'm not mistaken?"

Demetrius could hardly sit astride his horse now, the embarrassment was so excruciating. His lord was right, and wrong. It was marvellous that he should recall so trivial a thing as the girl Demetrius loved, so how could Demetrius point out that he'd progressed to another maiden? "I *did* favour Helena in my extreme youth. Happily I lived to see a true beauty before we embarked against the Amazons, and throughout our long months it has been true beauty I have dreamt on, true beauty that has whipped my soul almost to frenzies of adoration, true …" He stopped himself abruptly. "Not when I was preparing for battle, of course. I mean to say …"

The lord's horse sidestepped and gave an impatient snort, reminding the impulsive youth that a lesson had been about to be delivered. He bit his tongue and lowered his head. After a suitably impressive silence the great lord said distinctly:

"I see stone."

Several ambitious young knights had quietly brought up their horses to take the pressure off their friend and grab a share in any glory that might be in the offing. All hastily scanned the peaceful valley for stone. One noticed it in the wall around the olives and pointed there; another saw a few rocks on the plain and thought it conceivable that

They gasped, a little confusedly, for all they saw was that one rude hovel had walls of rough stone blocks instead of sticks and stuff, and that before its mean entrance two wonky branches made a petty kind of porch, thatched with straw.

Related Readings

a galloping horse might stumble and unseat its illustrious rider.

Demetrius redeemed himself by seeing what he was supposed to see. "I have it! That cottage!"

The others saw it now. They gasped, a little confusedly, for all they saw was that one rude hovel had walls of rough stone blocks instead of sticks and stuff, and that before its mean entrance two wonky branches made a petty kind of porch, thatched with straw.

"Tell me, Demetrius, now your eye has cleared—say why an unhappy fellow lives there."

"I cannot, my lord."

"Nor I," admitted two or three honest knights, knowing their lord valued candour and occasionally rewarded it.

"Gentlemen, you see in this innocent valley of ours the work of one who has ceased to offer thanks, one dissatisfied with his lot, one who has seen visions perhaps and been transported from his proper sphere of modest content. He has attempted to create for himself a palace, gentlemen, and has meant no doubt to install himself a king of currant bushes, emperor of olives and alders, lord of the larch, the laurel and the lazy stream!"

One elderly knight actually fell off his horse at this, he laughed so heartily. Mirth spread rapidly until all but the sullen captives of the barred wagons were shriek-ing and roaring at the ludicrous prospect, so obvious now it had been pointed out.

"It is funny to us," the lord admonished them gently when he sensed the initial flood diminishing, "but the matter is as grave as if it affected our very Court. These hapless outdwellers are simple folk but we have a duty towards them; they are stubborn for refusing to come live within the city walls, but we shall not abandon them for that. I say there is a man, albeit a peasant, who has misplaced even that tiny degree of command which was his birthright—he no longer knows himself but believes he is some other, greater man. Yet that cannot be. No man can be more than his birth provides for. The unhappiness his pride has caused him, or must soon cause him, touches me to the quick. Demetrius, and you, you, and you—go now into the valley and pull down that pompous stonework! And take care!" He threw the last phrase up and paused until all attention returned to him instead of the dancing horses and the merry diversion. "Take care—I do not want the little fellow harmed, nor his wife if he has a wife, nor his children if he has children. I want only the illusion removed, neatly as the bee-sting, and, to the same end, for we are coming home and shall protect *all* our people, even from those miseries so secret they do not suspect them."

"He has attempted to create for himself a palace, gentlemen, and has meant no doubt to install himself a king of currant bushes, emperor of olives and alders, lord of the larch, the laurel and the lazy stream!"

This great lord, who was not more than moderately vain and who really longed to go down in history as a just statesman rather than a raunchy club-man, was the legendary Theseus, son of the man whose name became a sea.

The stone place, which soon collapsed in upon itself with a dusty puff of silent smoke, far below, causing a patter of applause to break from the watchers on the high road, this stone place had been built by a weaver. And this weaver's father had once helped the legendary Theseus. And neither Theseus nor the weaver's father knew it. Theseus, for example, never thought to ask who had woven the marvellous thread that helped him through his greatest youthful exploit, to the heart of the labyrinth, the death of the Minotaur, and back again. And the old weaver, for example, never thought to ask just what the adamantine thread was for. All he did was pass on to his son a vision, a vision of a rare foreign beauty coming out of the forest one night with the gold from which the twine was to be fashioned. The vision was Ariadne. The weaver's son grew up believing that a similar vision would in due course come his way too.

This young, hearty, optimistic weaver, who lived in the forest a secluded but never a lonely life, was Nick Bottom. ■

Is the character of Theseus, as established by Watson, consistent with Shakespeare's portrayal of Theseus in the play? What characteristics are similar? Which are different?

In describing the owner of the stone hovel, Theseus expresses a view similar to the one he expresses in the famous speech about the imaginations of the lunatic, the lover, and the poet which opens Act Five in the play. Read the two pieces carefully and, in groups, discuss the similarities.

In a short composition, explore how Shakespeare's play can be seen as extending naturally from the comments made in the last two paragraphs of this selection.

Related Readings

by Aurand Harris

Robin Goodfellow

According to folklore, Puck or Robin Goodfellow began his
life as a mortal but was changed into a fairy by Oberon.
In this selection, American dramatist Aurand Harris
(b. 1915) recreates Robin's transformation and ends where
Shakespeare's story begins.

[There is a bare stage, typical of the time of Shakespeare....
There is soft light and forest music. Robin Goodfellow
enters from the side or up the aisle. He is a happy young
fellow, carefree and full of tricks.]

ROBIN: I have walked up a hill and down a hill,
Betwixt a hill, and thither I walk still.
If perchance you wonder whither and why,
"I'm out to find my fortune," answer I.
    [Intimately.]
When I was born, 'tis said fairies came
And called me "Robin Goodfellow" which is my name.
And a gypsy did foretell, as the moon waxed yellow,
Wonderous things would hap to Robin Goodfellow.
    [Walks.]
I'm out to find my fortune, where ere it be.
Perchance tomorrow it will befall to me!
    [Yawns.]
This night, this grassy knoll I'll use for sleeping.
No pillow—no cover spread—'tis in keeping.
    [Sits.]
O moon and stars who twinkle as you meet,
Behold me beneath—shivering—with cold feet.
    [Lifts bare feet and wiggles toes.]
'Twould be good fortune if I had but a shoe;
So dreaming of my fortune, good-night to you.

[Robin lies back, asleep. Fairy music is heard and the lights change in beautiful colored patterns. Oberon enters. He and all the fairies are dressed in shades of green.... He moves, almost dancing, cautiously to Robin, sees him, spins in a happy whirl.... Oberon pantomimes a pillow for Robin's head. Cobweb watches questioningly, then nods his head excitedly, and whirls to the side, snatching a pillow covered with leaves which is held off stage, and continuing to whirl, returns to Robin and places it under his head. Oberon pantomimes a cover to spread over Robin. Cobweb nods and whirls to side where he snatches a small cover of vine-net with flowers, and never missing a turn, he whirls back to Robin. He puts the cover over him, leaving two bare feet exposed. Oberon points to them and pantomimes shoes. Cobweb holds up two fingers, but Oberon already enjoying his own joke, holds up one finger for one shoe. Cobweb gets one small green shoe from the side and puts it on one foot. The foot immediately starts kicking in the air. Oberon points and shakes his finger at the shoe. The foot stops.... Oberon waves his hand three times and pulls from his sleeve a scroll of parchment. Oberon points and Cobweb puts the scroll by Robin's head. There is a faint sound of "Cook-a-doodle-do" off. Oberon and Cobweb listen and look. The rooster crows again. They nod and Oberon waves away Cobweb who runs and disappears between the curtains at back.... Oberon spreads and waves his arms in farewell, and exits at side in a whirl. Cobweb peeks out and quickly runs to Robin.... Cobweb quickly puts a second shoe on Robin's bare foot.... The rooster gives a long and final crow and the sun brightens the stage just as Cobweb escapes safely at side. Fairy music stops. Robin sits up, yawns and stretches, then opens his eyes in wonderment.]

ROBIN: I had a dream. Fairies did come and dance;
　　　　One wore a crown—King Oberon, perchance! *[Rises.]*
　　　　Methought a flower-cover they gently spread —
　　　　　　[Surprised, sees cover, holds it up, then drops it.]
　　　　Methought a leafy pillow cradled soft my head—
　　　　　　[Surprised, sees pillow, picks it up.]
　　　　I'll prove if this be a dream or this be true—*[Afraid to look.]*
　　　　They did set upon each foot a shoe. *[Slowly looks at feet,
　　　　　　sees and points at shoes and jumps with joy.]*
　　　　Ho, ho, ho, the owl hoots. *[His feet dance a sprightly jig.]*

My feet doth wear a pair of fairy boots.
And—in my dream methought I spied
A scroll neatly bound around and tied;
On it great words should be writ,
Which will explain, and all will fall to fit. *[Looks and sees scroll.]*
Ah, 'tis here, embraced with hair and fern.
And now these wonderous haps the why I'll learn.
> *[Opens scroll.]*
'Tis writ in letters bold—and each in gold!
I'll quick compound it. My curiosity feed.
> *[Starts to read, stops.]*
Forsooth, I forgot. I cannot read.

OBERON: *[Off, his voice is clearly heard as if through a megaphone.]*
Look and listen, behold and know,
Here with is writ to Robin Goodfellow.

ROBIN: 'Tis for me. Be it so.

OBERON: Harken ye, each fairy and elf—

ROBIN: A magic scroll that reads itself!

OBERON: I, King Oberon, do decree—

ROBIN: King Oberon speaks to *me!*

OBERON: To trick and tease thou hast cunning shifts
Which I'll encrease with other gifts.

ROBIN: O tricks I like to play, I wis!
I was sent away from home for this.

OBERON: Thou will have from this hour
Fairy magic and fairy power.

ROBIN: Fairy tricks to do? Magic power, too?

OBERON: Wish what thou wilt, it shall be thine.

ROBIN: Wish what I want and it is mine?

OBERON: Invisible you can be, or change your shape
To horse, to hog, to dog, to ape.
Transformed thus by fairy rules,
Reward the good and trick the fools. *[Robin nods.]*
Do thus and all the world will know
The name of Robin Goodfellow.
> *[Thinking it is the end of the message,*
> *Robin starts to roll up the scroll.]*
And if——*[Robin quickly unrolls scroll.]*
——thou keep my just command,
YOU with me will come and see Fairy Land!

ROBIN: *[Rolls up scroll and drops it on grassy knoll.]*
Blessed I am by fairies! King Oberon himself
Hath promised may be I'll be his jester elf!

And——[*In great wonder.*]
——if I follow his command
I—a mortal—will see Fairy Land!
He said, make a wish. That I'll do.
I'll make a wish and see if it comes true.
I wish—but with what wish should I begin?
I wish——[*Feels stomach.*]
—for FOOD for I am fain thin within.

> [*He closes his eyes. Magic music plays as Cobweb*
> *enters from side, puts food into Robin's hand, and*
> *exits. Music stops. He opens his eyes.*]

'Tis here! 'Tis true! O fairies where ere you be,
My stomach doth a full thanks give to thee.

> [*Swallows the dainty food in one bite.*]

I can be—invisible, he promised me.
Or—change my shape, to dog or ape, he stated.
Therefore, hear me, I will be translated!
First I'll be— first I'll try   to fly.
A bird I'll be and thither into the sky.

> [*He mimes this with great noise and joy, as he does the*
> *following with comic actions and sounds.*]

I wish to be—
A bee—a flea—
A bear—a chair—
A cat—a rat—
An owl, who-who—
A cow, moo-moo—
A frog—a dog—
A monkey with a tail—
The wind, a gale——[*Stops.*]
A tree with a little nest
So I——[*Pants.*]
—can take a rest.

In groups, prepare dramatic readings and pantomimes of this scene. Videotape your performance if you wish. In preparing and presenting your performance, it is not necessary to memorize the speeches. You may improvise or rewrite the dialogue using your own words.

Write a short scene dramatizing one of Robin's jests. Either research one of the stories told in the many books detailing the adventures of Robin Goodfellow or base your scene on what Puck says about himself in the play.

The scene ends with Robin's "I wish to be" sequence. Write your own version of his concluding speech.

Related Readings

by Nimmi Rashid

These two poems, both having roots in A Midsummer Night's
Dream *and its flowers, were written almost two centuries apart.
The first one is by Nimmi Rashid (b. 1979), a student from
Calgary, Alberta, and the other is by English Romantic poet John
Keats (1795–1821).*

Midsummer Night Flowers

Midsummer night flowers dance in the moonlight
like ballet dancers on a stage.
Petals float to earth
like fluttering fairy wings,
as green stems stand tall
like soldiers in a disordered row.
And the leaves which shelter fairies
are pillows upon which
dreaming children lay their sleepy heads.
The bright dew glistens
reflecting the slivered moon in the midnight sky
Fairies dance on cowslip ears,
intoxicated
with the sweet savour of musk roses.
The night flowers
wave in this magical night of the middle summer's spring.

Related Readings

by John Keats

I Cannot See What Fowers Are at My Feet

I cannot see what flowers are at my feet,
　　Nor what soft incense hangs upon the boughs,
But, in embalmed darkness, guess each sweet
　　Wherewith the seasonable month endows
The grass, the thicket, and the fruit-tree wild;
　　White hawthorn, and the pastoral eglantine;
　　　　Fast fading violets cover'd up in leaves;
　　　　And mid-May's eldest child,
The coming musk-rose, full of dewy wine,
　　　　The murmurous haunt of flies on summer eves.

Was it a vision, or a waking dream?
　　　　Fled is that music:—Do I wake or sleep?

from "Ode to a Nightingale"

Both poems depend on imagery for their effect—vivid descriptions that appeal to the senses. Write your own descriptive poem about some aspect of Shakespeare's fairy world, including imagery that appeals to a variety of senses.

EGLANTINE

OXLIPS'

WOODBINE

by Harry Harrison

A *Fragment* OF MANUSCRIPT

American science fiction writer Harry Harrison (b. 1925)
adds new meaning to Theseus' observation:

This is the greatest error of all the rest.
The man should be put into the lantern.
How is it else the man in the moon?

(5.1.243–45)

I found the two fragments of parchment, tied together with a bit of leather cord, behind one of the older bookcases in the Bodleian Library in Oxford. It was just chance. I had dropped a fifty pence bit—a heavy British coin bigger than a half dollar and worth eighty-five cents—and it had rolled into the gap between the bookcase and the wall. I could see it but could not reach it, so I pushed the bookcase a bit in order to get my hand in. I then reached the coin easily enough, but at the same time something slid down and struck against my fingers. I drew it out, along with the fifty pence, and it proved to be the parchment fragments referred to above.

In all truth I can lay no claims as to their authenticity, as to the authenticity of the writer that is, though their undoubted great age has been verified by certain chemical tests. If they are what they appear to be, lost lines from the Immortal Bard's own pen, they are indeed priceless and cast the light of knowledge upon some heretofore unsuspected aspects of his plays.

The chronology is clear enough. Ludovico Ariosto wrote *Orlando Furioso* in the early 1500s, and it is a well-known fact that Spenser took it as his model for *The Faerie Queene*. This was a common practise and Shakespeare himself drew on other books for the material for most of his plays. Since he wrote *A Midsummer Night's Dream* in the late 1500s there is every chance that he might have been acquainted with Ariosto's work, one of the earliest science fiction romances about a visit to the moon. Might Shakespeare not have decided to utilize the same idea? There is every possibility that the fragments of manuscript, a copy of which is appended below, will throw some light on this question.

A MIDSUMMER NIGHT'S DREAM

Act Three, Scene 1—The wood.

Enter Quince, Snug, Bottom, Flute, Snout, and Starveling.

BOTTOM: Are we all met?

QUINCE: Pat, pat; and here's a marvelous convenient place for our rehearsal. This green plot shall be our stage, this hawthorn-brake our tiring-house; and we will do it in action as we will do before the duke.

BOTTOM: Peter Quince,—

QUINCE: What sayest thou, Bully Bottom?

BOTTOM: There are things in this comedy of Lunar Man that will never please. First, landeth here a spatial ship, with roar and bluster; which the ladies cannot abide. How answer you that?

SNOUT: By'r lakin, a parlous fear.

STARVELING: I believe we must leave the rocket out, when all is done.

BOTTOM: Not a whit: I have a device to make all well. The thought of rockets we must disabuse, we for a stellar barque a null-G ship will use.

SNOUT: Will not the ladies be afeard of the null-G?

BOTTOM: Nay, indeed, a device so divers simple, a whipstock here to clutch and guide the course, and there above stout wainropes to hold secure and effect the landing in the proper place.

QUINCE: What place?

BOTTOM: Behind a wall, where ropes may be unhooked and secret means of flight thus be concealed.

SNOUT: You can never bring in a wall. What say you Quince?

QUINCE: No, in truth, we could not.

BOTTOM: Some man or other must present wall: and let him have some plaster, or some loam, or some rough-cast about him, to signify wall. But enough: this detail is but wrangle, we must press on. The Lunar Man shall step forth, around the wall of course, and there before the gathered nobles speak his speech.

QUINCE: What speech?

BOTTOM: Wit! whither wander you, the speech that we did copy from the book, chained there in church. How Lunar Man sailed safe the sea of space, with cunning coils did achieve null-G and, with parlous speed, escape velocity.

QUINCE: Escape from whom?

BOTTOM: Puisny knave did you not read? Escape from Earth, from Moon I mean, the first, then later burst the fairy bonds so insubstantial yet so firm that held we are upon this globe to death from birth.

QUINCE: But how? These raveled knots of thoughts do give amazement to my poll.

BOTTOM: I'll give amazement to your back, bat-fowling, bibble-babble mewling Quince, what is not clear?

QUINCE: All.

Bottom strikes Quince who falls. Exeunt severely.

A scrawled note across the last lines of the manuscript reads: *No, will not do, the market still unripe for SF. Rewrite—fantasy still best. Must buy book of fairy tales.*

ই ই ই

The narrator maintains that Ariosto's *Orlando Furioso* was "one of the earliest science fiction romances about a visit to the moon." Research other stories written in the 16th and 17th centuries that deal with flights to the moon, summarizing the basic plots of two or three of these stories. Is there any one story that you would prefer to read? Explain why.

In a short paragraph, explain why you think science fiction and fantasy books are read by people today. How do you feel about these genres? Would you consider Shakespeare's *A Midsummer Night's Dream* to be fantasy? Explain.

Hermia

by Sarojini Shintri

*Hermia has had her critics over the years. However, in her
study of women in Shakespeare's plays, Indian scholar
Sarojini Shintri comes to her defence.*

In a play like *A Midsummer Night's
Dream*, in which the supernatural element
so much dominates the human action—so
much so that love, that forms the backbone
of the story, can be inspired and reversed at
the least whim or fancy of the king of the
fairies, firm and detailed delineation of
character cannot justly be expected. The
play introduces us into a sort of a moonlit
[scene], where

> *By paved fountain or by rushy brook,*
> *Or in the beached margent of the sea,*
> *(2.1.85-86)*

the fairies dance their ringlets to "the
whistling wind," and marvels are to be
expected, being as it were native to these
regions. In such surroundings—which
throw their glamour on the story as well as
on its human agents, lulling one's moral and
critical perceptions—one comes across
Hermia and Helena with their stories to
enact.

They are both young and inexperienced.
They have stepped out of the seminar only
to find themselves exposed to the tender
mercies of love. They, in school—

> *... like two artificial gods,*
> *Have with our needles created both*
> *one flower,*
> *Both on one sampler, sitting on one*
> *cushion,*
> *Both warbling of one song, both in one*
> *key,*
> *. . . . .*
> *... So we grew together,*
> *Like to a double cherry, seeming*
> *parted,*
> *But yet an union in partition,*
> *(3.2.204–10)*

Still they differ in their temperaments as
much as in their appearance.

Hermia is out for emancipation, but, if
unsuccessful, she is prepared for the
worst—

> *So will I grow, so live, so die, my lord,*
> *Ere I will yield my virgin patent up*
> *Unto his lordship, whose unwished*
> *yoke*
> *My soul consents not to give*
> *sovereignty.*
> *(1.1.81-84)*

Related Readings

This expresses her strength of will and iron determination, and also her love of freedom. In addition, she has patience. The thought that "the course of true love never did run smooth" is a comfort to her—

> If then true lovers have been ever
> crossed
> It stands as an edict in destiny.
> Then let us teach our trial patience,
> Because it is a customary cross,
> (1.1.152-55)

And when Lysander suggests they should steal out of Athens, she welcomes the idea…. So she swears—

> … My good Lysander,
> I swear to thee, by Cupid's strongest
> bow,
>
> . . . .
>
> In that same place thou hast appointed
> me,
> Tomorrow truly will I meet with thee.
> (1.1.171-81)

Warburton has taken objection to her swearing thus. He writes: "Lysander does but just propose her running away from her father at midnight, and straight she is at her oaths that she will meet him at the place of rendezvous. Not one doubt or hesitation, not one condition of assurance for Lysander's constancy…." Warburton is grossly mistaken in his conception of the whole situation. Heath has well answered him: "Lysander asks no oaths of her. They are the superfluous but tender effusion of her own heartfelt passion…. She finely insinuates to her lover that … she loves him with a passion above being restrained by this or any other consideration…." One may add that her oaths are the expression not only of her joy but of her triumph. She can now defy the Athenian law and cross her father's purpose.

Being herself crossed in love, she has sympathy for Helena. The conversation between them [1.1.195–206] has led critics to think that Hermia, being herself well-beloved, is proud of her situation and wishes to impress on Helena her own superiority. This is unjust to Hermia. In fact, she has no reason to be cruel to Helena. Her words, "His folly, Helena, is no fault of mine," carry the heaviness of her heart. Her being loved by two men at once has not been to her, as Helena considers it, an unmixed boon.

Next, we see Hermia in the woods with Lysander. Then begins her trial. She sleeps in the confidence that Lysander is there by her side to guard her, but wakes up from a bad dream to find him no more near her.

Then takes place a most undignified "scolding match," as Mrs. Mackenzie calls it. Hermia's carriage all through this scene has been severely criticised. Charlton writes: "Her temper is as sharp as is her tongue, and excites itself most touchily in matters of her stature and her complexion. She was a vixen when she went to school, and even in the drawing rooms of the politer world, she has not quite mastered her instinct to bring her nails into the fray." But Hermia deserves better treatment. Charlton seems to have failed to understand the whole situation. It is natural that a weak and timid girl like Helena should consider her friend, who is more alive, bold and quick, a vixen. And Hermia's conduct in the first part of the play does not give us any reason to think her a virago; on the other hand, it is courageous, dignified and wholly admirable. So, her rudeness in this scene is to be attributed rather to the sad and helpless plight in which she finds herself than to her own true nature.

Leaving her kith and kin behind, she has come to the wood trusting in the

strongest assurances of her lover's fidelity. For her, there is no going back to Athens except at the peril of her life. The only alternative left to her is to follow Lysander. Not so is Helena's case. There is nothing to prevent her going back to Athens. There is no law against her. But Hermia is an outlaw. So, how would she feel when she hears her own dear love speak thus?—

> LYSANDER: *Why seek'st thou me? Could not this make thee know,*
> *The hate I bear thee made me leave thee so?*
>
> > *(3.2.190-91)*

Only then comes Helena's passionate chiding—

> HELENA: *Lo, she is one of this confederacy!*
>
> . . . .
>
> *Injurious Hermia, most ungrateful maid!*
> *Have you conspired, have you with these contrived*
> *To bait me with this foul derision?*
>
> > *(3.2.193-98)*

Her reaction is—

> *I am amazed at your passionate words.*
> *I scorn you not; it seems that you scorn me.*
>
> > *(3.2.221-22)*

Helena's charges do not tear an impatient repartee from her tongue. But when Lysander shows earnestness in his avowal of love for Helena and detestation of herself, the true nature of the situation dawns upon her mind—

> *Hate me? Wherefore? O me! What news, my love?*
> *Am not I Hermia? Are not you Lysander?*
> *I am as fair now as I was erewhile.*
> *Since night you loved me; yet since night you left me.*
> *Why, then you left me—O, the gods forbid!*
> *In earnest, shall I say?*
>
> > *(3.2.278-83)*

And Lysander's cruel answer—

> *Ay, by my life;*
> *And never did desire to see thee more.*
> *Therefore be out of hope, of question, of doubt.*
> *Be certain, nothing truer. 'Tis no jest*
> *That I do hate thee and love Helena.*
> > *(3.2.284-88)*

quite naturally makes her desperate and fierce. She then suspects Helena and calls her a "juggler" and a "canker blossom," while the repeated reference to her short stature and dark complexion makes her mad.

If jealousy can make men monsters, fickleness and fraud on the part of men whom they love, might make spirited women act like furies.

Hermia is not "by nature a shrew," as Furnivall has tried to show. Nor is she a vixen; but a young spirited woman, lively, and independent in thought. She is a *revoltée*.... And when she, already in the bad books of her father, finds herself lonely and deserted by all—even by Lysander himself whom she has passionately loved and wholeheartedly trusted,—the hope that she had revelled in, that she can go away and marry Lysander and thus defy the Athenian law, and the strength that had sustained her so long give way, and she becomes exasperated and desperately fierce. But once she gets back her Lysander, the rest is silence.

Before judging her conduct in that one scene, one has to take into consideration the fairies' intervention. The juice of the flower has the potency to change a lover's eyes. Lysander's alienation is externally motivated; and Hermia, Helena, Lysander, and Demetrius are completely ignorant of this. So, what ensues after the fairy charm has been exercised, is a comedy of errors threatening to resolve itself into a tragedy. And a comedy of errors is not a good criterion of character; because the character itself is misled in its understanding and judgement. It is interesting to consider here that Shakespeare made use of the flower called "love-in-idleness" as a symbol. Perhaps, he wants to point out that lovers' hearts are fickle and that one needs only sufficient provocation to betray one's true character. ■

According to Shintri, what are Hermia's best qualities? To what extent do you agree with Shintri's view of Hermia's character? Explain fully.

Using Shintri's analysis as a model, write a full character sketch of Helena.

Create a collage illustrating the various facets of Hermia's character as outlined by Shintri. Briefly explain your choice of pictures and how they relate to the character traits.

TO PUCK

by Beatrice Llewellyn Thomas

In a tribute to one of Shakespeare's most memorable creations, English poet Beatrice Llewellyn Thomas suggests why we are in such need of characters like Puck.

I hear you, little spirit, in the bushes,
 Laughing where the heather blossoms low,
Where the tiny fieldmouse softly pushes
 Nose inquisitive and eyes aglow.
Little sprite of laughter and derision,
 Tender-hearted spirit of good luck,
Pranking through the dream of days Elysian,
 Teach me laughter, Puck!

Puck, you elf, you wisely merry fairy,
 What have you to do with solemn men?
You so foot it, airiest of airy,
 That we only catch you now and then.
Earnest, sombre-browed, we follow after
 You, who fly a-mocking from the ruck;
O we have a desperate need of laughter!
 Give us laughter, Puck!

Write a paragraph in response to the thought expressed in the last two lines of the poem.

Write your own poem to Puck. Find or create an illustration to accompany your poem.

Forgotten Dreams

by Edward Silvera

In Romeo and Juliet *we are told that there is nothing more insubstantial than a dream. When the four lovers awake at the end of Act Four, they share the sentiment expressed in the following poem written by American poet Edward Silvera (1906-1937).*

The soft gray hands of sleep

Toiled all night long

To spin a beautiful garment

Of dreams;

At dawn

The little task was done.

Awakening,

The garb so deftly spun

Was only a heap

Of ravelled thread—

A vague remembrance

In my head.

Write your own poem about the illusive quality of dreams. Find or create an illustration to accompany your poem.

by Norrie Epstein

A Most Rare Vision

In this essay, Norrie Epstein, American author of The Friendly Shakespeare *(1993), discusses the "deep truths" in* A Midsummer Night's Dream.

Like a dream itself, *A Midsummer Night's Dream* presents a startling mixture of disparate elements: homely and realistic characters are placed within a fantastic, almost surrealistic, plot; the lowest level of society mixes with the highest; prosaic speech is uttered along with sublime poetry; and the supernatural, the human, and the bestial worlds commingle. And, like a dream, this dramatic fairy tale initially appears to be a trivial diversion that bears little connection to our waking lives. Yet, upon closer examination, *A Midsummer Night's Dream* reveals, in disguised form, deep truths about our hidden emotional life.

In *A Midsummer Night's Dream* Shakespeare does something with his two central pairs of lovers that he had never done before and would do only once again (with Rosencrantz and Guildenstern in *Hamlet*): he creates characters who are interchangeable—a striking departure for a playwright who usually distinguishes every character, no matter how minor. Lysander loves Hermia, and Hermia, Lysander; Demetrius also loves Hermia; and Helena, odd woman out, is infatuated with Demetrius. But any combination would serve the purposes of the plot. No matter how many times you read this play, you'll get Hermia and Helena confused. The only difference between them is that one is tall,

the other short; they are the stock lovers found in any romantic comedy—except that, this being Shakespeare, they speak more beautifully. The same is true of the men: Lysander could suddenly become Demetrius and the audience would never be any the wiser. That's precisely Shakespeare's point; this play, which deals in magic, illusion, and enchantment, is about the mysterious power of love to transform an ordinary mortal into a rarity of perfection:

> *Things base and vile, holding no quantity,*
> *Love can transpose to form and dignity.*
> *Love looks not with the eyes, but*
> *with the mind ...*
> *(1.1.235–37)*

But since we aren't under the lovers' spell, we see them with the cool eyes of reason, and they all look alike to us. And apparently to Puck as well. When Oberon orders him to sprinkle "love juice" in the eyes of an Athenian man, he mistakes Lysander for Demetrius, the intended recipient. Thus Lysander, once passionate about Hermia, is now deeply in love with Helena. Then, to rectify his error, Puck squeezes the juice onto Demetrius, and he, too, falls for the once-despised Helena. Love, long recognized as a form of enchantment, literally becomes a spell.

Modern audiences tend to resist the idea of magic, but many Elizabethans still believed in fairies, only their creatures were much darker and more sinister than the bland images manufactured by Walt Disney. Their traditional habitat, the dark forest where confused travelers lose their way, belongs more to the strange tales of the Brothers Grimm. Shakespeare's moon-drenched fairy world is a symbolic dreamscape where traditional distinctions blur and disappear. By entering the enchanted woods at nightfall, the lovers abandon the familiar daylight world, as represented by civilized Athens, and enter a mental landscape, a covert realm within the unconscious, a place of fearsome transformations and self-discovery. Just as insanity, poetry, and dreams possess their own fantastic logic, revealing an unsettling yet truthful vision of ordinary life, so the dark woodlands—as seen in countless myths and fairy tales—expose the flip side of civilization, revealing the tenuous boundary that distinguishes reason and madness, lust and love.

Although the characters have transferred their affections, the situation remains the same: Hermia is merely exchanged for Helena....

Meanwhile, there are other visitors to the forest that night. The Athenian tradesmen have gathered there to rehearse the "tedious brief scene of young Pyramus and Thisbe," which they intend to perform for Duke Theseus in honor of his forthcoming nuptials. As he watches them rehearse, Puck snickers at their amateurish bungling, just as he mocks the inanity of the young lovers: "Shall we their fond pageants see? / Lord, what fools these mortals be!" ("Fond" meant foolish.) From Puck's superior perspective, the mortal world is a ridiculous farce, and he laughs at the confused lovers just as later the lovers will snicker at the artisans when they put on *their* show....

But the fairy kingdom is not immune to disorder. In Oberon and Titania's bitter feud, the theme of love's delusion is carried to an even darker extreme. Enraged at Titania's refusal to give him her beloved Indian boy,

Oberon sprinkles the love juice in Titania's eyes while hissing this malediction:

> *What thou seest when thou dost wake,*
> *Do it for thy true-love take;*
> *Love and languish for his sake.*
> *Be it ounce, or cat, or bear,*
> *Pard, or boar with bristled hair,*
> *In thy eye that shall appear,*
> *When thou wak'st, it is thy dear.*
> *Wake when some vile thing is near!*
>
> (2.2.26–33)

Unfortunately, it's the newly "translated" Bottom who, thanks to Puck's mischief, is now crowned with the head of an ass....

... In *A Midsummer Night's Dream* the ordinary question, "What does she (or he) see in him (or her)?" is taken to an extreme: Who among us, Shakespeare seems to ask, hasn't fallen for an ass and believed him (or her) a god?

And who, upon awakening from the enchantment of love, has not been embarrassed to discover the mistake?

Released from her spell, Titania shudders, half remembering, not quite certain of what she has done, or if what has happened is real or an illusion. Similarly, the lovers, their confusion dispelled by Puck and Oberon, fall into a deep sleep and wake never knowing if their experiences have been a vision or reality. Perhaps a little of both. As Hermia says: "Methinks I see these things with parted eye, / When everything seems double." Exhausted by their ordeal, they all "to Athens back again repair, / And

think no more of this night's accidents, / But as the fierce vexation of a dream." Demetrius still retains the effects of the love potion, leaving us to wonder if his love for Helena is "real"; but as Shakespeare has already shown us, all love—even "true" love—is a form of sorcery. And, after all, this is a comedy, and everyone must get married.

All the different plots and social strata come together in the final scene, when the artisans assemble before lovers and nobles to put on their play in honor of the weddings. Scholars believe that *A Midsummer Night's Dream* was written to grace the marriage of a noble couple, so in essence, Shakespeare's original audience watched a play that contained a play that was watched by courtiers. The levels of deception and mirror images in this play are astonishing, and it's easy to get trapped amid all the shimmering reflections. Ironically, it's the oafish Bottom who has the wisest comment on the night's experiences, and students and scholars of Shakespeare would do well to pay attention:

> *I have had a most rare vision. I have had a dream, past the wit of man to say what dream it was. Man is but an ass, if he go about to expound this dream.*
>
> (4.1.207–10) ∎

In a short paragraph, respond to one of the "deep truths" revealed in *A Midsummer Night's Dream*. If you prefer, write your response in the form of a letter to Norrie Epstein.

In her conclusion, Epstein refers to "levels of deception and mirror images." What does she mean by this? Write a short paragraph exploring your response to her view.

PYRAMUS and THISBE

*The most lamentable comedy that Peter Quince has
chosen for his actors to play before the Duke is based on a myth
made popular by the Latin poet Ovid in his book
Metamorphoses (c. A.D. 8). In this book, Ovid tells a series of
fanciful stories that explain how things in nature were transformed
into their present appearance. Ovid's tale is retold here by
American classicist Edith Hamilton (1867–1963).*

Once upon a time the deep red berries of the mulberry tree were white as snow. The change in color came about strangely and sadly. The death of two young lovers was the cause.

Pyramus and Thisbe, he the most beautiful youth and she the loveliest maiden of all the East, lived in Babylon, the city of Queen Semiramis, in houses so close together that one wall was common to both. Growing up thus side by side they learned to love each other. They longed to marry, but their parents forbade. Love, however, cannot be forbidden. The more that flame is covered up, the hotter it burns. Also love can always find a way. It was impossible that these two whose hearts were on fire should be kept apart.

In the wall both houses shared there was a little chink. No one before had noticed it, but there is nothing a lover does not notice. Our two young people discovered it and through it they were able to whisper sweetly back and forth, Thisbe on one side, Pyramus on the other. The hateful wall that separated them had become their means of reaching each other. "But for you we could touch, kiss," they would say. "But at least you let us speak together. You give a passage for loving words to reach loving ears. We are not ungrateful." So they would talk, and as night came on and they must part, each would press on the wall kisses that could not go through to the lips on the other side.

Every morning when the dawn had put out the stars, and the sun's rays had dried the hoarfrost on the grass, they would steal to the crack and, standing there, now utter words of burning love and now lament their hard fate, but always in softest whispers. Finally a day came when they could endure no longer. They decided that that very night they would try to slip away and steal out through the city into the open country where at last they could be together in freedom. They agreed to meet at a well-known place, the Tomb of Ninus, under a tree there, a tall mulberry full of snow-white berries, near which a cool spring bubbled up. The plan pleased them and it seemed to them the day would never end.

At last the sun sank into the sea and night arose. In the darkness Thisbe crept out and made her way in all secrecy to the tomb. Pyramus had not come; still she waited for him, her love making her bold. But all of a sudden she saw by the light of the moon a lioness. The fierce beast had made a kill; her jaws were bloody and she was coming to slake her thirst in the spring. She was still far enough away for Thisbe to escape, but as she fled she dropped her cloak. The lioness came upon it on her way back to her lair and she mouthed it and tore it before disappearing into the woods. That is what Pyramus saw when he appeared a few minutes later. Before him lay the blood-stained shreds of the cloak and clear in the dust were the tracks of the lioness. The conclusion was inevitable. He never doubted that he knew all. Thisbe was dead. He had let his love, a tender maiden, come alone to a place full of danger, and not been there first to protect her. "It is I who killed you," he said. He lifted up from the trampled dust what was left of the cloak and kissing it again and again carried it to the

mulberry tree. "Now," he said, "you shall drink my blood too." He drew his sword and plunged it into his side. The blood spurted up over the berries and dyed them a dark red.

Thisbe, although terrified of the lioness, was still more afraid to fail her lover. She ventured to go back to the tree of the tryst, the mulberry with the shining white fruit. She could not find it. A tree was there, but not one gleam of white was on the branches. As she stared at it, something moved on the ground beneath. She started back shuddering. But in a moment, peering through the shadows, she saw what was there. It was Pyramus, bathed in blood and dying. She flew to him and threw her arms around him. She kissed his cold lips and begged him to look at her, to speak to her.

"It is I, your Thisbe, your dearest," she cried to him. At the sound of her name he opened his heavy eyes for one look. Then death closed them.

She saw his sword fallen from his hand and beside it her cloak stained and torn. She understood all. "Your own hand killed you," she said, "and your love for me. I too can be brave. I too can love. Only death would have had the power to separate us. It shall not have that power now." She plunged into her heart the sword that was still wet with his life's blood.

The gods were pitiful at the end, and the lovers' parents too. The deep red fruit of the mulberry is the everlasting memorial of these true lovers, and one urn holds the ashes of the two whom not even death could part. ■

Many myths can be seen as attempts by earlier civilizations to make sense of the world. Describe some other myths that serve the purpose of explaining some element in nature. Do you think our ancient ancestors believed these stories? Explain.

Most myths have a moral lesson to teach. What lessons can be derived from this story?

Related Readings

A World UPSIDE Down

by Marchette Chute

*According to American historian Marchette Chute (b. 1909),
A Midsummer Night's Dream appeals to the audience because it is like
"looking at the world upside down."*

A Midsummer Night's Dream is all moonlight, with a touch of moonshine. It is the most enchanting fairy tale ever written and yet it reflects with cheerful fidelity the villagers and cowslips and hedgehogs of the ordinary English countryside. It is like looking at the world upside down in a sheet of water. All the familiar things are there but, like Bottom, they are translated.

No one but Shakespeare would have set someone like Bottom in fairyland. For Bottom was a weaver and of a practical nature, and in any other hands but Shakespeare's he would have trampled on the delicate fabric of the play. But Bottom, helpfully instructing a fairy how to attack a "red-hipped humble-bee on the top of a thistle" and the exact way to carry home the honey-bag, shows a bland dignity that is quite undisturbed by the fact he happens at the moment to be ornamented with an ass's head and a wreath of musk-roses.

A Midsummer Night's Dream reaches its climax in the play that is acted before Duke Theseus, with Bottom heading the cast. All England was in the grip of these well-intentioned local amateur theatricals, which seemed even funnier then than they do now; for the old plays that were still being acted had a stiff elegance and an impassioned melancholy that made them a little ridiculous even when they were properly presented. A play like *Appius and Virginia* was advertised as a "tragical comedy" and its long lines wailed like a defective bagpipe.

> *O man, O mould, O muck, O clay!*
> *O hell, O hellish hound.*
> *O false Judge Appius, rabbling*
> *wretch, is this thy treason found?*

It needed only the most delicate touch to push this sort of thing into the realm of outright comedy, and Shakespeare supplied it in the "very tragical mirth" of Bottom's conscientious production of Pyramus and Thisbe. The gallant little troupe in their solemn performance before Duke Theseus present the funniest tragedy that ever brought tears of helpless mirth to the eyes of the audience.

Shakespeare had used the device before ... but what had been merely charmingly effective in the earlier play becomes a comic masterpiece in the *Dream*. Yet, however Shakespeare may smile at Bottom and his earnest fellow actors, the great actor-dramatist did not really feel superior to them. "The best in this kind are but shadows, and the worst are no worse, if imagination amend them." It is part of Shakespeare's great strength as a writer that he never felt superior to anyone, and he kept a gentle courtesy in his point of view even towards fools.

This same gentleness on Shakespeare's part shows in his attitude towards the earlier writers from whom he took the plots of some of his plays. He could pick up a rather foolish play or poem, read it with great care, ignore its foolishness for the little of value there might be in it, and then transform it into a masterpiece. ■

Write a short composition to expand the comparisons Chute draws in the first paragraph.

What does Chute find appealing about Bottom's character? Do you agree with her conclusions? Explain.

To what extent do you agree with Chute's opinion that Shakespeare "kept a gentle courtesy in his point of view even towards fools"? What evidence is there in the play that Shakespeare was kind to Bottom and his friends or, on the other hand, that he used this play to ridicule amateur actors?

Related Readings

by Northrop Frye

The Bottomless Dream

*Despite its unconventional plot and odd assortment of characters,
A Midsummer Night's Dream fits into a long tradition of comedy.
According to Canadian scholar and critic Northrop Frye (1912-91),
Shakespeare's play conforms to the three-part archetypal pattern of
comedy established by the ancient Greeks.*

This play retains the three parts of a normal comedy ...: a first part in which an absurd, unpleasant or irrational situation is set up; a second part of confused identity and personal complications; a third part in which the plot gives a shake and twist and everything comes right in the end. In the opening of this play we meet an irrational law, of a type we often do meet at the beginning of a Shakespeare comedy: the law of Athens that decrees death or perpetual imprisonment in a convent for any young woman who marries without her father's consent. Here the young woman is Hermia, who loves Lysander, and the law is invoked by her father, Egeus, who prefers Demetrius. Egeus is a senile old fool who clearly doesn't love his daughter, and is quite reconciled to seeing her executed or imprisoned. What he loves is his own possession of his daughter, which carries the right to bestow her on a man of his choice

as a proxy for himself. He makes his priorities clear in a speech later in the play:

> They would have stolen away, they
>   would, Demetrius,
> Thereby to have defeated you and me.
> You of your wife, and me of my con-
>   sent,
> Of my consent that she should be
>   your wife.
>   (4.1.157-160)

Nevertheless Theseus admits that the law is what Egeus says it is, and also emphatically says that the law must be enforced, and that he himself has no power to abrogate it.... As it turns out that Theseus is a fairly decent sort, we may like to rationalize this scene by assuming that he is probably going to talk privately with Egeus and Demetrius (as in fact he says he is) and work out a more humane solution. But he gives Hermia no loophole: he merely repeats the threats to her life and freedom. Then he adjourns the session:

> Come my Hippolyta, what cheer my love?

> (1.1.124)

which seems a clear indication that Hippolyta, portrayed throughout the play as a person of great common sense, doesn't like the set-up at all.

We realize that sooner or later Lysander and Hermia will get out from under this law and be united in spite of Egeus. Demetrius and Helena ... are in an unresolved situation: Helena loves Demetrius, but Demetrius has only, in the Victorian sense, trifled with her affections. In the second part we're in the fairy wood at night, where identities become, as we think, hopelessly confused. At dawn Theseus and Hippolyta, accompanied by Egeus, enter the wood to hunt. By that time the Demetrius Helena situation has cleared up, and because of that Theseus feels able to overrule Egeus and allow the two marriages to go ahead. At the beginning Lysander remarks to Hermia that the authority of Athenian law doesn't extend as far as the wood, but apparently it does; Theseus is there, in full charge, and it is in the wood that he makes the decision that heads the play toward its happy ending. At the same time the solidifying of the Demetrius-Helena relationship was the work of Oberon. We can hardly avoid the feeling not only that Theseus is overruling Egeus's will, but that his own will has been overruled too, by fairies of whom he knows nothing and in whose existence he doesn't believe.

If we look at the grouping of characters in each of the three parts, this feeling becomes still stronger. In the opening scene we have Theseus, Egeus and an unwilling Hippolyta in the centre, symbolizing parental authority and the inflexibility of law.... In the second part the characters are grouped in different places within the wood, for the most part separated from one another.... In the first part no one doubts that Theseus is the supreme ruler over the court of Athens; in the second part no one doubts that Oberon is king of the fairies and directs what goes on in the magic wood.

In the third and final part the characters, no longer separated from one another, are very symmetrically arranged. Peter Quince and his company are in the most unlikely spot, in the middle, and the centre of attention; around them sit Theseus and Hippolyta and the four now reconciled lovers. The play ends; Theseus calls for a retreat to bed, and then the fairies come in for the final blessing of the house, forming a circumference around all the others. They are there for the sake of Theseus and Hippolyta, but their presence suggests that Theseus is not as supremely the ruler of his own world as he seemed to be at first. ■

In describing the three parts of comedy, Frye suggests that different characters exert their power and authority. Outline the major points in Frye's analysis in this regard. To what extent do you agree with his analysis? Explain.

In this selection, Frye offers a number of interesting, undeveloped observations regarding the character and/or motivation of Egeus, Hippolyta, and Theseus. Identify these undeveloped observations and discuss in more detail the opinions suggested by Frye.

Related Readings

by David Garrick

SONG—*for* *Epilogue*

English actor and playwright David Garrick (1717–79) wrote and produced popular "improved" versions of Shakespeare's work for enthusiastic audiences. Garrick's versions retained much of the original poetry, but scenes, dialogue, and songs were added. In 1763 Garrick presented his version of A Midsummer Night's Dream, *featuring an Epilogue, which, in Shakespeare's version, Bottom and his crew are not permitted to present.*

QUINCE: Most noble Duke, to us be kind;
Be you and all your courtiers blind,
That you may not our errors find,
    But smile upon our sport.
For we are simple actors all,
Some fat some lean, some short, some tall;
Our pride is great, our merit small;
    Will that pray, do at court?

STARVELING: The writer too of this same piece,
Like other poets here of Greece,
May think all swans, that are but geese,
    And spoil your princely sport.
Six honest folk we are, no doubt,
But scarce know what we've been about,
And tho' we're honest, if we're out,
    That will not do at court.

BOTTOM: Shall tinkers, weavers, tailors, dare
  To strut and bounce like any player,
  And show you all, what fools we are,
   And that way make you sport?
  Our lofty parts we could not hit,
  For what we undertook unfit;
  Much noise indeed, but little wit,
   That will not do at court.

FLUTE: O would the Duke and Duchess smile,
  The court would do the same awhile
  But call us after, low and vile,
   And that way make their sport:
  Nay, would you still more pastime makc,
  And at poor we your purses shake,
  Whatever you give, we'll gladly take,
   For that will do at court.

   ða ða ða

Write an additional verse for this song from the point of view of Snout or Snug.
Makc it consistent with the role he plays in the Pyramus and Thisbe scene.

Imagine you are directing Shakespeare's *A Midsummer Night's Dream* and the
suggestion is made that Garrick's Epilogue be included. Write a short dialogue or
composition in which you discuss the reasons for or against including it in your
production.

Related Readings

by Charles Harpur

A Midsummer Noon in the Australian Forest

*Australian poet Charles Harpur (1813–68) recreates the rhythm
and tone of the closing speeches of the play to evoke the
atmosphere of a midsummer noon in the forest.*

Not a sound disturbs the air,

There is quiet everywhere;

Over plains and over woods

What a mighty stillness broods!

All the birds and insects keep

Where the coolest shadows sleep;

Even the busy ants are found

Resting in their pebbled mound;

Even the locust clingeth now

Silent to the barky bough:

Over hills and over plains

Quiet, vast and slumbrous, reigns.

Only there's a drowsy humming

From yon warm lagoon slow coming:

'Tis the dragon-hornet—see!

All bedaubed resplendently,

Yellow on a tawny ground—

Each rich spot nor square nor round,

Rudely heart-shaped, as it were
The blurred and hasty impress there
Of a vermeil-crusted seal
Dusted o'er with golden meal.
Only there's a droning where
Yon bright beetle shines in air,
Tracks it in its gleaming flight
With a slanting beam of light,
Rising in the sunshine higher,
Till its shards flame out like fire.

Every other thing is still,
Save the ever-wakeful rill,
Whose cool murmur only throws
Cooler comfort round repose;
Or some ripple in the sea
Of leafy boughs, where, lazily,
Tired summer, in her bower
Turning with the noontide hour,
Heaves a slumbrous breath ere she
Once more slumbers peacefully.

O 'tis easeful here to lie
Hidden from noon's scorching eye,
In this grassy cool recess
Musing thus of quietness.

Write your own descriptive poem. Choose a familiar location and use the rhythm
pattern established by Puck and Oberon at the end of Act Five and recreated by
Harpur in his poem. If possible, include images and details from *A Midsummer
Night's Dream*.

by Mary Ellen Lamb

The Myth of Theseus and the Minotaur

Is A Midsummer Night's Dream merely a light comedy, intended to entertain, or is there a darker, more serious side to the work? American scholar Mary Ellen Lamb discusses this topic in the following selection.

According to Golding's Ovid and North's Plutarch, two texts often consulted by Shakespeare, this myth includes the following account: the minotaur was a monster half bull and half human.... King Minos directed Daedalus to construct an intricate labyrinth to contain this creature, which was fed with human flesh. Included among the minotaur's victims were youths, both male and female, offered periodically as tribute to Crete from conquered Athens. These unfortunates were placed in the labyrinth, where they were doomed to wander until they starved to death, or until they were consumed by the minotaur. One year, King Aegeus's son Theseus asked to be included in this tribute. When he arrived at Crete, King Minos's daughter Ariadne fell in love with him and provided him with a thread to tie at the entrance of the labyrinth so that he could find his way out. Having vowed his love for Ariadne, Theseus killed the minotaur and, as agreed, took her with him when he escaped Crete. However, he broke his vow on the trip homeward and abandoned her as she slept on an island where the ship had docked. Most of the details of this myth appear in one way or another in *A Midsummer Night's Dream*.

The labyrinth itself, in which Athenian youth are sacrificed to the minotaur, contains broad implications for *A Midsummer Night's Dream*. Like the youth of the myth, the young lovers of the play enter a kind of labyrinth, a forest where they become hopelessly lost; and at the center of this labyrinth is a creature, half human and half ass. The similarity between the forest of the play and the labyrinth becomes even more striking when the myth is understood according to the allegorical reading of the day: the minotaur's labyrinth represented vice, ... in which sinners lose themselves until aided by some external power. This allegorical understanding of the labyrinth provides a new context for the lovers' progressive "loss" of themselves in their own passions as the play progresses. They enter the forest-labyrinth with a purpose: Hermia and Lysander are fleeing to Lysander's aunt's house, where they will be free to marry; Demetrius is pursuing his beloved Hermia, somehow to prevent her from marrying Lysander; and Helena is pursuing Demetrius "to have his sight

thither, and back again" (1.1.254). By the end of their sojourn in the forest, however, their motives of love have changed to more violent impulses as they circle each other helplessly, Demetrius and Lysander attempting to slay each other for love of Helena, Helena fleeing Hermia's sharp nails. Like the sinners of the allegorical interpretation, they are unable to save themselves; and it is only through the beneficent aid of the fairies that they emerge, alive and evenly paired, back where they began.

The presence of Bottom as the minotaur adapts the Theseus myth to the comic spirit of the play. Yet Bottom is also a creature of the Theseus myth, and his identity as a comic minotaur extends beyond the fact that he is half human and half ass.

At the time [the] name "bottom" was used to refer to "thread" or "a skein of thread," the household item which played a crucial role in delivering Theseus from the labyrinth. In fact, Caxton's translation of the *Aeneid* uses the exact phrase "a botom of threde" in the description of Theseus's adventure with the minotaur. Furthermore, Bottom's vocation as a weaver would bring the association of this meaning of his name to the mind of an Elizabethan audience.

Bottom is both the monster of this labyrinth and the thread leading the way out of it; and the complexity of our response to him is demonstrated by the widely differing attitudes adopted towards him. On the one hand, Bottom is truly an ass; in fact, he is called an ass twice in the course of the play. Surrounded by magic and moonshine, lying in the arms of the fairy queen, yet oblivious to her considerable charms, Bottom asks only to be fed "your good dry oats" and to be scratched about the face, where he is "marvellous hairy" (4.1.32, 24).... On the other hand, into his braying mouth are placed the wisest sentiments about love expressed in the play. He knows that he is not the paragon Titania admires; when she compliments his beauty and wisdom, his reply shows an honest sense of his own limitations: "Not so, neither" (3.1.138). Unlike the other characters, he knows that "reason and love keep little company together, now-a-days" (3.1.133–34). In short, Bottom is an ass because he does not succumb to love; and he is a thread out of this labyrinth because he refuses to abandon his common sense even in Titania's embrace. Chasing a rival through a nettle-filled forest would never be for him.

The substitution of Bottom for a minotaur represents the transmutation of the elements of tragedy into comedy. And the close relationship between comedy and tragedy was a problem Shakespeare was exploring in, for example, the farcical production of Pyramus and Thisbe, "very tragical mirth" (5.1.59). In fact, Pyramus's humorous invocation to the Furies to "cut thread and thrum" (5.1.282), deflating grand tragic style by reminding his audience that he is really a weaver at heart, glances at the implications of the myth for tragedy: one can become lost and die in a labyrinth without a thread to lead the way out. This is, in a way, what happens to

> *Bottom is both the monster of this labyrinth and the thread leading the way out of it; and the complexity of our response to him is demonstrated by the widely differing attitudes adopted towards him.*

Pyramus and Thisbe; in the force of his passion, Pyramus leaps to a false conclusion about Thisbe's death, and both lovers commit impulsive suicide. This hilarious short play reminds us of a dark truth: under different circumstances the Athenian lovers, who were also escaping a forbidding father by running into the woods, might also have perished.

Of course, *A Midsummer Night's Dream* remains a very funny comedy, and its dark side should not be overstated. ■

According to Lamb, many details of the Theseus myth appear in *A Midsummer Night's Dream.* Summarize briefly the role that the labyrinth, the Minotaur, and the ball of thread play in Shakespeare's comedy. To what extent do you agree or disagree with Lamb's interpretation? Explain.

Lamb suggests that Bottom is the key to understanding the allegorical implications of the play. What does she mean by this? Write a composition in which you explore Bottom's role and character in the play.

Related Readings

by Roo Borson

After Dark the Flowers

In this prose poem, Canadian author Roo (Ruth Elizabeth) Borson (b. 1952) describes an unforgettable night full of magic and mood, darkness and dreams.

After dark the flowers let their other scent into the air, as if thinking aloud. Wild roses, magenta and white, the white ones their furred ghosts. And the wheedling music of the insects, planning a city that was never meant to come to fruition in daylight. What dreamers they are. And yet, just listening to them, that glittering bank of lights comes back: whatever city you imagined first, in childhood, as the way in or out.

We went, didn't we, each of us, after something. Like a dog running after a stick which was nothing more than the faked motion of his master's throwing arm. We lost what we couldn't remember. We lost our intentions.

The stars approach, but only so near they don't ground themselves on the shallows. They let their cargo be unloaded from them. And what cargo they carried, back in those days! The hotel, white as an iced cake among the palms. The palms, their bark that fell away like netting, the fronds we'd find like huge whips on the ground after a storm.

All night the pines grow electric with insect noise: enough power for a whole city. But the barest beginning of dawn shuts them down, so the insects wait in silence and limbo beneath the bark as another personality takes over the earth. One with a baby blue sky and the pines twisted against it in the shapes of our old, powerful, outmoded longings. ■

This selection is much more than a poetic description of the night. The evocative language appeals as much to the senses as it does to the imagination. Write your own prose poem describing the fairyland forest from the point of view of any character in the play.

Related Readings

by Richard Armour

Ill Met by Moonlight

Here is a retelling of the play A Midsummer Night's Dream *like you have never read before. To Richard Armour, nothing is sacred—including Shakespeare!*

In the woods, Puck (alias Robin Goodfellow) and a Fairy meet. Puck is a merry sprite with quite a reputation for what he considers screamingly funny pranks, like hiding in people's drinks to give them an extra kick, or pretending to be a chair and upsetting the occupant. It's his job to keep Oberon, King of the Fairies, in stitches.

"How now, spirit," asks Puck, "whither wander you?"

"Over hill, over dale, through brush, through briar, over park, over pale, through flood, through fire," says the Fairy, obviously a letter carrier whom nothing stays from completion of his (or her) appointed rounds. At the moment, however, the Fairy is busy looking for dewdrops, hanging pearls in cowslips' ears, and doing other odd jobs you would have to be a fairy to appreciate.

Oberon, with his train, and Titania, the Fairy Queen, with her train, enter from opposite directions.[1] Oberon and Titania have been sleeping in separate acorn cups, because Titania has a young lad among her attendants whom Oberon wants her to give up. It may be that Oberon suspects he isn't really a fairy.

"Ill met by moonlight," says Oberon grumpily when he sees his wife. He enjoys his moonshine more when she isn't around.

They exchange some sharp words, Titania charging Oberon with having an affair with Hippolyta (which Oberon, in view of his size, is hardly up to), and Oberon insinuating that Titania has been dallying, and possibly dillying, with Theseus (who couldn't see her without a magnifying glass). Overcome by jealousy, they don't realize how small they are being.[2]

---

1. The place is beginning to look like Grand Central Station.

2. Because of a shortage of actors only a half-inch tall, the Fairies are usually played by ordinary-sized people.

After Titania leaves with her train in a huff (and a chuff, chuff), Oberon plots to discomfit her, leaving her without a comfit to her name. He orders Puck, who can go anywhere in a trice,[3] to hustle off and fetch a certain flower, the juice of which, when rubbed on the eyelids of a sleeping person, will make him fall madly in love with the next creature he sees.[4] The trick, of course, is to rub the sleeper's eyelids without waking him.

"I'll put a girdle round about the earth in forty minutes," boasts Puck, zooming off with a corset in his hands.

Left to himself, Oberon chuckles about how he will use the juice of the flower on Titania when she is asleep, and how she will then fall in love with the first creature of the forest she sees on waking....

When Puck returns with the magic flower, Oberon takes it from him and, without so much as a thank you, launches upon a famous speech.

"I know a bank where the wild thyme blows," he says, all the while running the flower through a juicer, "where oxlips and the nodding violet grows." There, he is certain, Titania will be found nodding with the violets. He ... hies to the bank, where he believes Titania to be deposited.

Oberon sneaks in and drops some juice on her eyelids, hoping the first thing she sees when she wakes is something good and repulsive, like an ounce, a pard, or a bore with rough whiskers.

When he arrives, Titania is getting ready for bed. "Sing me now asleep," she commands, and the fairies sing a lullaby that knocks her out as effectively as a sleeping pill. While she is slumbering, Oberon sneaks in and drops some juice on her eyelids, hoping the first thing she sees when she wakes is something good and repulsive, like an ounce,[5] a pard, or a bore with rough whiskers.

Shortly afterward Quince, Bottom, and the rest of the mechanicals assemble in the woods to rehearse their play. Luckily for the plot, they pick a place close to where Titania lies sleeping, and Puck is watching them from behind some bushes.

"What hempen homespuns have we swaggering here, so near the cradle of the Queen?" Pucks asks himself. Always up to some prank, he puts an ass's head on top of Bottom when he is offstage, and when the weaver comes in to recite his lines, the rest of the players flee in terror.

The first thing Titania sees when she awakens is Bottom. "What angel wakes me from my flowery bed?" she cries in ecstasy. "Come, sit thee down upon this bed, while I thy amiable cheeks do coy, and stick musk-roses in thy sleek smooth head, and kiss thy

---

3. A Fairy tricycle.

4. What would happen if one eye were anointed and the other not, is thought-provoking.

5. A pound would be even better.

Related Readings

fair large ears." She can't seem to get over those ears of his—not without a ladder.

Bottom takes it all in stride, not being one to question his good fortune, even when Titania gives him four fairies named Peaseblossom, Cobweb, Moth, and Mustardseed.[6] They take care of his every-day wants, such as feeding him apricocks, fetching him jewels from the deep, and fanning moonbeams from his eyes. Bottom has never had such service before, even at the annual weavers' clambake.

"Let's have the tongs and the bones,"[7] he suggests. And then, when thirst overtakes him, he calls for "a bottle of hay," perhaps planning to drink it through a straw.

Finally Bottom and Titania lie down on a bed of flowers, from which the thorns and thistles have been carefully removed. Bottom accepts everything nonchalantly, though he complains mildly that there are no sheets. "Sleep thou, and I will wind thee in my arms," says Titania soothingly.

While they sleep, Oberon, who is watching from a thicket, dances with wild Abandon[8] and laughs hysterically....

Oberon begins to feel sorry for his fairy wife, Titania, and touches her eyes, mean-while chanting, "Be thou as thou wast wont to be." She wonts to be awake, and very shortly is.

When she is shown the sleeping Bottom, of whom she has been so enamored, Titania is mortified. Even after his ass's head is removed, there is little improvement.

"Sound, music!" cries Oberon. "Come, my queen, take hands with me, and let's rock the ground." Then Oberon and Titania dance what is probably the first rock and roll, and afterward promise to be friends forevermore, even though married. As dawn is about to break, the fairies get out of there. They know how silly they look in the daylight, and anyhow need to rest up for the next night's shenanigans. ■

---

6. These *could* be nicknames, let us hope.

7. "Crude musical instruments," according to the authorities. Apparently the bones were picked up with the tongs, to avoid using one's fingers.

8. A disreputable friend of his.

In retelling the story of *A Midsummer Night's Dream*, Armour uses puns and wordplays. Choose three puns that you think are especially clever and another three that you would classify as "groaners." Explain the wordplay in any three of the puns you have chosen.

Write to Richard Armour, expressing your opinion about the value of his work being used in a classroom setting.

In groups, prepare a dramatic (comical) presentation of any scene as retold by Armour. Your reading should emphasize the wordplay and intelligent silliness of the selection.

On Accepting Enchantment

by Margaret Webster

According to American actress and director Margaret Webster (1905-72), "Enchanted woods have been with us from the earliest fairy stories we learned as children"—and the greatest challenge for directors is to persuade the audience to accept the enchantment. To accomplish this, a number of traditions have been established. Here are just a few of them.

A Midsummer Night's Dream is as moon-drenched as *Romeo and Juliet* is shot with stars. The moon is not in a malignant phase, but her radiance sheds a disturbing magic this midsummer night, holding all the play in an opalescent enchantment, where everything seems "translated." Only with Theseus' hunting horns at dawn and the music of his hounds does the thin, silver mist dissolve and a world emerge in which lovers are mortal ..., trees are trees merely, and Bottom can scratch his ear without the inexplicable feeling that it has grown long and hairy. Not until *The Tempest* will Shakespeare write a play with elements as delicately ethereal as these.

How are we to translate them into terms of scenery? The old traveling companies used to rise blithely above the problem, with a green drop vaguely bedecked with painted foliage and two or three wooden backboards covered with dusty grass-matting. They probably served the play as well or better than more ambitious producers have done. It is perilously easy to obliterate this fragile fairyland behind a stageful of massive scenery, elaborate, fantastical, and unnecessary. Our wood must be a mood, an atmosphere, where anything may happen, gauzes, perhaps, silhouettes and shadows, light, transparent, fluid—a wood of dreams.

If only the fairies also could be made of gossamer! I have sometimes wondered whether we could disembody all of them, except Oberon, Titania, and Puck, using the heliograph principle to produce dancing points of light, mirror-reflections flashing and darting like will-o'-the-wisps. Shakespeare presented his "fairies," as he later did his witches, according to the conventions of the day, and in following this lead we are generally forced to rely on the talents of the nearest available dancing school. But we must not ignore the drawbacks of the thumping of little feet. It is more important to keep the verse on tiptoe, quivering and agleam, than to indulge in dainty ballets by "fairies" who are vocally flat-footed.... There is nothing very difficult for the actors in this play. We are apt to discount the lovers, with a secret fear that they are a bore, and to let the clowns loose with free, galumphing feet. The lovers need not be wearisome, though, admittedly, the women are better than the men. Both Helena and Hermia are vivid enough and tartly contrasted. If our "Helena" will play a rather silly girl in love as a rather silly girl in love, and not moan for our sympathy all the time, she will be fully rewarded by our surprised delight when the worm turns and upbraids her dearest friend with all the armory of feminine cattiness assured of male support. There is some very elegant fooling in the quarrel scene between the quartet.

Nor need Demetrius and Lysander ... accept the usual fate of stooges, if they will play for the enchantment of the wood and make us realize the depths of bemused and driveling sentimentality to which its magic

There is nothing very difficult for the actors in this play. We are apt to discount the lovers, with a secret fear that they are a bore, and to let the clowns loose with free, galumphing feet.

has reduced two ordinarily upstanding and normal young men. In the play's first and last scenes they are both drawn lightly but quite firmly; what they establish in these scenes will govern the degree of comedy to be extracted from their moonlit aberrations....

For the lovers, more clearly even than Theseus and Hippolyta, form the link between the honest, tangible, homespun craftsman's world, peopled by the so-called clowns, and the airy dimension which Oberon and Titania inhabit. Puck knows both worlds and partakes of them. But to him the mortal world represents every reasonable idea standing idiotically on its head; whereas, to the lovers and clowns, Titania's domain dissolves all reliable and stable values in fluidity and bewilderment. Bottom, of course, is the most deeply entangled, and in him the most solid of the earthy elements is enmeshed by the most delicate fabric of the fairy world.

The clowns are straightforward stuff. They are apt to emerge a trifle encrusted with tradition, which has gathered as thick as barnacles around them. There is, for instance, one piece of business still in common use, whereby Thisbe, bent on self-destruction, falls on Pyramus' scabbard instead of on his sword. This seems to date right back to the original production, for it is described by a member of the Elizabethan audience. Since then, over the centuries, directors and comedians have wrung every shred of opportunity out of the Pyramus

and Thisbe interlude; their inventions have been preserved in the memory of succeeding actors and handed on, with additions.

Many of them remain genuinely, if not very subtly, funny. The director must select judiciously, and above all, keep the fooling spontaneous and not allow it to stretch out interminably in order to include everybody's notion of a "comic" touch.... "Simpleness and duty" are accredited to the amateur actors [5.1.87], and the fun will be heightened if they do remember that they are supposedly playing to the Duke and his companions and do not too freely caricature the traditions of village-hall theatricals. The scene offers limitless possibilities. We may treat it with temperance and do nobody any harm.

In other scenes than this the Clowns are dogged with tradition. Starveling is supposedly deaf. When he is told that he is to play Thisbe's mother, he has for generations interpolated: "Thisbe's brother?" *"Mother!"* replies the united troupe. Flute has immemorially protested that he has "a beard—" "Huh?" from his companions, "—coming!" But the Clowns are genuine, human, and indestructible. We fall for them today as they did in Elizabethan London. This is a lighthearted, irresponsible piece of mischief and magic; let us lend our best ears to its melodies and warm our hearts at its humanity. The moonlit Shakespearean heavens will not often be so beautifully cloudless, nor his lyric gift of song so purely melodious. ■

Webster describes a number of traditions that have developed in the staging of this play. Choose any two and write a composition defending or criticizing the continuation of these traditions.

What other staging problems does the play present? If you were the director, how would you deal with these difficulties?

The Curtain

by Guy Boas

Guy Boas (1896–1966) provides a glimpse of what happens when the curtain comes down and the dream is over. The shadows must make their way home—in their own way.

When the curtain goes down at the end of the play,
The actors and actresses hurry away.

Titania, Bottom and Quince, being stars,
Can afford to drive home in their own private cars.

Hippolyta, Starveling and Flute are in luck,
They've been offered a lift in a taxi by Puck;

And Snug and Lysander and Oberon pop
In a bus, and Demetrius clambers on top.

With a chorus of fairies no bus can compete,
So they are obliged to trudge home on their feet.

It seems rather hard on the poor little things,
After flying about all the evening with wings.

This poem has actors finding their way home. Write a poem, similar in style and tone, in which the same troupe of actors are in a different setting—for example, at a party or in a restaurant.

ABOUT THE SERIES EDITORS

Dom Saliani, Senior Editor of the *Global Shakespeare Series*, is the Curriculum Leader of English at Sir Winston Churchill High School in Calgary, Alberta. He has been an English teacher for over 25 years and has published a number of poetry and literature anthologies.

Chris Ferguson is currently employed as a Special Trainer by the Southwest Educational Development Laboratory in Austin, Texas. Formerly the Department Head of English at Burnet High School in Burnet, Texas, she has taught English, drama, and speech communications for over 15 years.

Dr. Tim Scott is an English teacher at Melbourne Grammar School in Victoria, Australia, where he directs a Shakespeare production every year. He wrote his Ph.D. thesis on Elizabethan drama.

REVIEWERS

The publishers and editors would like to thank the following educators for contributing their valuable expertise to the development of the *Global Shakespeare Series*:

Nancy B. Alford
Sir John A. Macdonald High School
Hubley, Nova Scotia

Philip V. Allingham, Ph.D.
Golden Secondary School
Golden, British Columbia

Francine Artichuk
Riverview Senior High
Riverview, New Brunswick

Robert M. Bilan
Oak Park High School
Winnipeg, Manitoba

Carol Brown
Walter Murray Collegiate Institute
Saskatoon, Saskatchewan

Rod Brown
Wellington Secondary School
Nanaimo, British Columbia

Beverley Calabrese
Minto Memorial High School
Minto, New Brunswick

Anne Carrier
Northern Secondary School
Toronto, Ontario

Joan Connell
Charlottetown Rural High School
Charlottetown, Prince Edward Island

Brian Dietrich
Queen Elizabeth Senior Secondary
Surrey, British Columbia

Alison Douglas
McNally High School
Edmonton, Alberta

Kimberley A. Driscoll
Adam Scott Collegiate
Peterborough, Ontario

Burton Eikleberry
Grants Pass High School
Grants Pass, Oregon

Gloria Evans
Lakewood Junior Secondary School
Prince George, British Columbia

Graham T. Foster
Calgary Catholic School District
Calgary, Alberta

Catherine Foy
Cobourg D.C.I. East
Cobourg, Ontario

Professor Averil Gardner
Memorial University
St. John's, Newfoundland

Doug Gregory
William E. Hay Composite High School
Stettler, Alberta

Joyce L. Halsey
Lee's Summit North High School
Lee's Summit, Missouri

Carol Innazzo
St. Bernard's College
West Essendon, Victoria
Australia

Winston Jackson
Belmont Secondary School
Victoria, British Columbia

Marion Jenkins
Glenlyon-Norfolk School
Victoria, British Columbia

Sharon Johnston, Ph.D.
Boone High School
Orlando, Florida

Jean Jonkers
William J. Dean Technical High School
Holyoke, Massachusetts

Beverly Joyce
Brockton High School
Brockton, Massachusetts

Judy Kayse
Huntsville High School
Huntsville, Texas

Doreen Kennedy
Vancouver Technical Secondary School
Burnaby, British Columbia

Betty King
District 3
Corner Brook, Newfoundland

Dan Kral
Regina Catholic School Education Centre
Regina, Saskatchewan

Ross Laing
Sir Wilfrid Laurier Secondary School
Orleans, Ontario

Kathryn Lemmon
James Fowler Senior High
Calgary, Alberta

Ed Metcalfe
Fleetwood Park Secondary School
Surrey, British Columbia

Janine Modestow
William J. Dean Technical High School
Holyoke, Massachusetts

Mary Mullen
Morell Regional High School
Morell, Prince Edward Island

Steve Naylor
Salmon Arm Senior Secondary School
Salmon Arm, British Columbia

Kathleen Oakes
Implay City Senior High School
Romeo, Michigan

Carla O'Brien
Lakewood Junior Secondary School
Prince George, British Columbia

Bruce L. Pagni
Waukegan High School
Waukegan, Illinois

Larry Peters
Lisgar Collegiate
Ottawa, Ontario

Margaret Poetschke
Lisgar Collegiate
Ottawa, Ontario

Jeff Purse
Walter Murray Collegiate Institute
Saskatoon, Saskatchewan

Grant Shaw
Elmwood High School
Winnipeg, Manitoba

Debarah Shoultz
Columbus North High School
Columbus, Indiana

Elaine Snaden
Windsor Board of Education
Windsor, Ontario

Tim Turner
Kiona-Benton High School
Benton City, Washington

Sylvia Unkovich
David Thompson Secondary School
Vancouver, British Columbia

James Walsh
Vernon Township High School
Vernon, New Jersey

Joan K. Wasserman
Lake of Two Mountains High School
Deux Montagnes, Quebec

Brian T.W. Way, Ph.D.
Oakridge Secondary School
London, Ontario

Kimberly Weisner
Merritt Island High School
Merritt Island, Florida

Edward R. Wholey
Sir John A. Macdonald High School
Halifax, Nova Scotia

Garry Williamson
Murdoch Mackay Collegiate
Winnipeg, Manitoba

Beverley Winny
Adam Scott Secondary School
Peterborough, Ontario

Thelfa Yee-Toi
Campbell Collegiate
Regina, Saskatchewan

ACKNOWLEDGMENTS

Permission to reprint copyrighted material is gratefully acknowledged. Every reasonable effort has been made to contact copyright holders. Any information that enables the publishers to rectify any error or omission will be welcomed. Selections may retain original spellings, punctuation, and usage.

Winter Moon by Langston Hughes from COLLECTED POEMS by Langston Hughes. Copyright © 1994 by the Estate of Langston Hughes. Reprinted by permission of Alfred A. Knopf Inc. and Harold Ober and Associates Incorporated. *On Seeing* A Midsummer Night's Dream by Henry Miller from THE HAMLET LETTERS, copyright © 1987 by Henry Miller. Reprinted with permission of Capra Press, Santa Barbara. *Theseus and the Unhappy Man* by Robert Watson from WHILOM by Robert Watson. First published in 1990. Copyright © 1990 by Robert Watson. Published by Bloomsbury Publishing Ltd. *Robin Goodfellow* by Aurand Harris from ROBIN GOODFELLOW, published by Anchorage Press, P.O. Box 8067, New Orleans, Louisiana, USA. *Midsummer Night Flowers* by Nimmi Rashid used by permission of the poet. *I Cannot See What Flowers Are at My Feet* by John Keats. Public domain. *A Fragment of Manuscript* by Harry Harrison. Copyright © 1997 by Harry Harrison. *Hermia* by Sarojini Shintri from *Women in Shakespeare* which appeared in RESEARCH PUBLICATION SERIES 32, Karnatak University, Dharwad, 1977. *To Puck* by Beatrice Llewellyn Thomas from THE HOME BOOK OF MODERN VERSE edited by Burton Egbert Stevenson, copyright © 1925 by Henry Holt and Company, Inc., copyright © 1953 by Burton Egbert Stevenson. Reprinted by permission of Henry Holt and Company, Inc. *Forgotten Dreams* by Edward Silvera from THE POETRY OF THE NEGRO 1746–1949. Published by Doubleday Publishing. *A Most Rare Vision* by Norrie Epstein from THE FRIENDLY SHAKESPEARE by Norrie Epstein. Copyright © 1993 by Norrie Epstein, Jon Winokur, and Reid Boates. Used by permission of Viking Penguin, a division of Penguin Books USA Inc. *Pyramus and Thisbe* by Edith Hamilton from MYTHOLOGY by Edith Hamilton. Copyright © 1940, 1942 by Edith Hamilton; © renewed 1969 by Dorian Fielding Reid and Doris Fielding Reid. By permission of Little, Brown and Company. *A World Upside Down* by Marchette Chute from INTRODUCTION TO SHAKESPEARE by Marchette Chute. Copyright © 1951, renewed © 1979 by Marchette Chute. Used by permission of Dutton Signet, a division of Penguin Books USA Inc. *The Bottomless Dream* by Northrop Frye from NORTHROP FRYE ON SHAKESPEARE, edited by Robert Sandler. Copyright © 1986 by Northrop Frye. Yale University Press, 1986, and Chelsea House Publishers. *Song—for Epilogue* by David Garrick. Public domain. *A Midsummer Noon in the Australian Forest* by Charles Harpur. Public domain. *The Myth of Theseus and the Minotaur* by Mary Ellen Lamb appeared in expanded form in TEXAS STUDIES IN LANGUAGE AND LITERATURE 21.4 (1979): 478–91. *After Dark the Flowers* by Roo Borson first appeared in THE WHOLE NIGHT COMING HOME, McClelland and Stewart, 1984. Reprinted by permission of the author. *Ill Met by Moonlight* by Richard Armour. Copyright © by Richard Armour. Reprinted by permission of John Hawkins & Associates, Inc. *On Accepting Enchantment* by Margaret Webster from SHAKESPEARE WITHOUT TEARS. Published by The World Publishing Company. *The Curtain* by Guy Boas reproduced by permission of Punch Ltd.

ARTWORK

Yuan Lee: cover, 16, 26–27, 30, 40–41, 46, 60–61, 70, 74–75, 82, 94–95; detail from *The Life and Death of Sir Henry Unton* (c. 1596) by courtesy of the National Portrait Gallery, London, 9; **Folger Shakespeare Library,** reprinted with permission: title page of *A Midsummer Night's Dream* from the First Quarto (1600), 10; first page of *A Midsummer Night's Dream* from the First Quarto (1600), 11; **John James:** a performance at the Globe Theatre from *Shakespeare's Theatre* (Simon and Schuster, 1994), 13; **Mike Reagan:** 14; **Nicholas Vitacco:** 15; **Allan Moon:** series logo; marginal art: 19, 33, 37, 38, 51, 84; Pyramus and Thisbe from Ovid, *Metamorphoses* (1538), 24; Phibbus' car from Hyginus, *Fabularum liber* (1549), 25; griffin from Giulio Cesare Capaccio, *Delle impresse trattato* (1592), 36; "And those things ..." from John Taylor, *Mad Fashions, Od Fashions* (1642), 56; bear-baiting from Charles Knight, *Pictorial Edition of the Words of Shakspere* (1839–43), 58; canker-blossom from John Johnstone, *Opera aliquot* (1650–62), 61; **Studio Bello:** 101, 133; **Pierre-Paul Pariseau:** 104; **Peter Ferguson:** 113, 115; **Tadeusz Majewski:** 121; **Thom Sevalrud:** 124; WH 48469 *Thisbe* by John William Waterhouse (1849-1917), Whitford & Hughes, London/Bridgeman Art Library Int'l Ltd., London/New York, 130; **Carmelo Blandino:** 141; **Michael Wertz:** 145; **Peter Lacalamita:** 151; **Russ Wilms:** 153.